Sunshine
for the
Latter-day
Saint
Soul

D0377982

Sunshine
for the
Latter-day
Saint
Soul

BOOKCRAFT
Salt Lake City, Utah

Library of Congress Catalog Card Number: 98-74082

ISBN 1-57008-580-3

Fourth Printing, 1999

Printed in the United States of America

Contents

Home and Family

Teaching by Example

Courage

Happiness and Gratitude

Service and Sacrifice

$\mathscr{P}$reface

$\mathbf{N}$one but the Saints can be happy under every circumstance," recorded the faithful and stalwart pioneer Eliza Roxcy Snow.

And in her quiet observation, Eliza R. Snow succinctly embodied a distinguishing feature of members of The Church of Jesus Christ of Latter-day Saints: they understand the plan, God's plan in fact, to allow each one of us the ability to achieve eternal life and exaltation with Heavenly Father and his Son, Jesus Christ.

Though heartaches, tribulations, suffering, and persecution may surround us, we have the ability to persevere through calling upon the peace and comfort that come from a loving Savior. Many times that feeling of peace, that moment of inspiration, may come through a lesson or talk we hear in church meetings or family home evening lessons. And it is often those few words that give us the ability to endure to the end or the motivation to do better. Those words are truly inspired in their ability to change our attitudes.

This book, *Sunshine for the Latter-day Saint Soul,* is just that—words of inspiration from talks, lessons, hymns, poems, and stories that have been told throughout the Church in sermons, magazine articles, books, and lessons. Thematically arranged, these stories include insight from President Boyd K. Packer on trusting in the Lord; lessons about humility and sacrifice from Elder Marion D. Hanks; a missionary's witness of the truthfulness of the Lord's work from Elder John H. Groberg; gospel principles taught through humor in the delightful words of George D. Durrant; and thoughts on the power of prayer from well-known speaker and author Anita R. Canfield.

This collection is truly a treasure trove of inspiring stories that will touch the soul of Latter-day Saint readers as they identify with the authors and recognize similar stories of faith, service, happiness, courage, and so on, in their own lives.

Bookcraft thanks the authors for allowing their timeless stories to be used in such a publication. Gratitude is also expressed to Lesley Taylor, Brad Olsen, and Tiffany Pack, who were among those that took so much time to read and reread the vast amount of available literature and pick from that assortment the 101 stories included here.

It is the publisher's hope that readers will find these stories to be inspiring and that the messages will bring sunshine to their souls.

Love
and
Compassion

"*I* Wuv You"

Anita R. Canfield

When our youngest child was two or three, my husband, Steve, took her with him to a thrift store that always carried old magazines and postcards. He placed her in the shopping cart, next to his side, as he thumbed through a stack of old magazines, looking for a specific issue. Intrigued and lost in thought, he was only slightly aware of her jabbering until he was jarred into reality as he realized she was trying to climb out of the cart.

With his attention now turned away from his cache of antiques, he began to focus on the object of her effort to be free.

She was pointing and talking in her toddler's jabber to a young man about ten feet away, an employee of the thrift store. Steve turned his full attention to Paige's chatter and tried to figure out what she wanted from this young man.

He immediately saw that this man had been in some kind of serious accident, probably a fire or burn accident. His legs were dragging limply behind him, an arm was severely burned and shriveled. His face and head had been so disfigured that the right side of his chin seemed to have melted into his neck. An ear, an eye, and most of his nose were gone. Only a few absurd tufts of hair remained impossibly among the screaming mass of bright red scar tissue. He was gruesome in appearance.

At first, Steve feared Paige's curiosity, concerned that she might offend the man. Then he soon realized it wasn't curiosity at all, she was trying to reach out to the man to give him a hug! He had been shaking his head at her trying to discourage her when finally he looked up at Steve as if to say, "What do I do?" Steve smiled and simply nodded his head in approval. The young man slowly shuffled closer to her as she reached out to hug him. Reverently, he just slightly touched her hand with his whole one. She grabbed his arm and hugged him unabashedly. Then she looked up at him, smiling and giggling like only a toddler can do, and said, "I wuv you!" Overcome with emotion, he quickly turned and walked away, brushing tears from his cheek.

After paying for his purchases, Steve noticed him standing near the front doors. He approached Steve and placed in his hand an old, very worn, green stuffed animal. His voice trembling with choking emotion he said, "Please, give this to her, and tell her someday what she meant to me."

"Thou Would Still Be Adored"

HOWARD W. HUNTER

You will remember the story of Thomas Moore, the famous nineteenth century Irish poet who was called away on a business trip. Upon his return he was met at the door not by his beautiful bride, but by someone who gave him the message that his wife was upstairs and had asked that he not come up. Then the poet learned the terrible truth. His wife had contracted smallpox during his absence and the disease had left her once flawless and beautiful face scarred and pocked with the disease. She had taken one look at her reflection in the mirror and commanded that the shutters be drawn and that her husband never see her again.

Thomas Moore would not listen. He ran upstairs and threw open the door of his wife's room, but the room was dark and she made no sound. As he went to turn on the lamp she cried out, "No, don't light the lamps. Please go, this is the greatest gift I can give you. Go now." He left the room and went downstairs to his study and sat up all night prayerfully thinking and composing not a poem, as he had before, but his first song. He not only wrote the words but he wrote the music.

The next morning, as soon as the sun was up, he returned to his wife's room and called out, "Are you awake?" She answered, "I am, but do not come in." He sang to his wife that song that we hear today on occasions:

> Believe me if all these endearing young charms,
> Which I gaze on so fondly today,
> Were to change by tomorrow and flee in my arms
> Like fairy gifts fading away,
> Thou would still be adored
> As this moment thou art
> Let thy loveliness fade as it will.

And then he heard a movement from the corner of the room where his wife lay in her loneliness, and he finished the song:

> Let thy loveliness fade as it will
> And around the dear ruin
> Each wish of my heart
> Would entwine itself verdantly still.

The song ended. She arose from her bed, crossed the room, and they fell into each other's arms.

A Father's Support

MARION D. HANKS

A young lad stood at the pulpit one Sunday trying to give an assigned talk, but he could not get the words out. His spiritual giant of a father walked from the congregation to stand beside his son, put his arm around him, and said: "I know Larry has prepared his talk and that he'll be able to give it. He is a little frightened, so I'll just speak to you for a moment and then I know he'll be ready." The father stood by his boy with his arm around him, and in a moment the lad gave his talk. And many in the congregation wept.

If I Can Stop One Heart from Breaking

EMILY DICKINSON

If I can stop one heart from breaking,
I shall not live in vain;
If I can ease one life the aching,
Or cool one pain,
Or help one fainting robin
Unto his nest again,
I shall not live in vain.

6

My Very Dear Sarah

SULLIVAN BALLOU

Editor's Note: While encamped with his unit just outside of Washington in July 1861, Union Major Sullivan Ballou of the 2nd Rhode Island Volunteers wrote a letter to his wife, Sarah. He was killed a week later during the First Battle of Bull Run, the first big engagement of the American Civil War (1861–65).

Camp Clark, Washington
July 14, 1861

My very dear Sarah,

The indications are very strong that we shall move in a few days—perhaps tomorrow. Lest I should not be able to write again, I feel impelled to write a few lines that may fall under your eye when I shall be no more. Our movements may be of a few days' duration and full of pleasure—and it may be one of some conflict and death to me. "Not my will, but thine, O God be done." If it is necessary that I should fall on the battlefield for my Country, I am ready.

I have no misgivings about, or lack of confidence in, the cause in which I am engaged, and my courage does not halt or falter. I know how strongly American Civilization now leans on the triumph of the Government, and how great a debt we owe to those who went before us through the blood and sufferings of the Revolution. And I am willing—perfectly willing—to lay down all my joys in this life, to help maintain this Government, and to pay that debt. . . .

Sarah, my love for you is deathless. It seems to bind me with mighty cables that nothing but Omnipotence could break; and yet my love of Country comes over me like a strong wind and burns me unresistibly on with all these chains to the battlefield.

The memories of the blissful moments I have spent with you come creeping over me, and I feel most gratified to God and to you that I have enjoyed them so long. And hard it is for me to give them up and burn to ashes the hopes of future years, when, God willing, we might still have lived and loved together, and seen our sons grown up to honorable manhood around us. I have, I know, but few and small claims upon Divine Providence, but something whispers to me—perhaps it is the wafted prayer of my little Edgar—that I shall return to my loved ones unharmed. If I do not, my dear Sarah, never forget how much I love you, and when my last breath escapes me on the battlefield, it will whisper your name. Forgive my many faults, and the many pains I have caused you. How thoughtless and foolish I have often times been! How gladly would I wash out with my tears every little spot upon your happiness, and struggle with all the misfortunes of this world to shield you and your children from harm. But I cannot. I must watch you from the Spirit-land and hover near you, while you buffet the storm, with your precious little freight, and wait with sad patience till we meet to part no more.

But, O Sarah! If the dead can come back to this earth and flit unseen around those they loved, I shall always be near you; in the gladdest days and in the darkest nights, advised to your happiest scenes and gloomiest hours, *always, always,* and if there be a soft breeze upon your cheek, it shall be my breath; as the cool air fans your throbbing temple, it shall be my spirit passing by. Sarah, do not mourn me dead; think I am gone and wait for thee, for we shall meet again.

As for my little boys—they will grow up as I have done, and never know a father's love and care. Little Willie is too young to remember me long, and my blue-eyed Edgar will keep my frolics with him among the dim memories of childhood. Sarah, I have unlimited confidence in your maternal care and your development of their character, and feel that God will bless you in your holy work.

Tell my two Mothers I call God's blessing upon them. O! Sarah. I wait for you there; come to me and lead thither my children.

Sullivan

*T*rue Beauty

ELAINE CANNON

My family and I were new in a neighborhood, and I had just met a fine gentleman with whom I'd be serving in a Church assignment. We were visiting in the foyer of the chapel when I asked him when I would get to meet his wife.

"Now," he said, "Why wait? You are in for a treat!"

"Wonderful," I returned. "Where is she?"

"She's in the cultural hall."

So were a dozen other women I didn't know yet, who were decorating for a church bazaar.

"How will I know her?"

"Easy!" He was exuberant. "Go in there and look for the most beautiful woman in the room—that's my wife." Then he gave me a few more details and I left. I entered the room look-ing for a lady who was a cross between Sophia Loren and a young Audrey Hepburn. What I saw were mothers of many, empty-nesters, and some fine Molly Mormons. I didn't see one who answered his descriptions at all. Finally I asked someone and she pointed out the man's wife.

As I think about this woman now, I can think only of beauty and loveliness. Honestly. I know her as one of the finest women I've ever met. I love her for her great kindness to me over the years. But at that moment I was shocked. There must be some mistake! Not only was the woman who had been pointed out to me no movie star but she also had few redeem-ing features. I noticed that she had gentle curls of fine ma-hogany hair, a light in her eyes, and a warm smile. But that was it. Her eyes were unusually wide set. Her lips were thick, sur-rounding an ugly overbite. Her ears were prominent. Her nose, however, was the nose of a movie-star—Bob Hope! But that smile and those eyes, when I introduced myself, obliterated im-perfect features.

Of course he loved her. He'd lived with her. He'd shared pillow talk. She had been told that she was beautiful and desirable so many times that *she was!* He'd been the object of her incredibly generous service and her unequivocal support. That woman would crawl through a forest of prickly trees and tangleweeds to help her man. Of course he loved her.

The Only Friend He Ever Had

GEORGE D. DURRANT

I know a man whose son was one of the most unusual and choice young men who ever lived. His warm smile and cheerful greeting caused many to love him. He knew how to goof off, but never in such a way that anybody got hurt. He knew how to have fun, but it was always clean fun. As the school years went by, he attracted many friends because of his positive and sincere attitude. In his last year of high school he was elected senior class president. But toward the end of that year, this fine young man, who had never been sick in his life, contracted a rare disease. Within a period of just ten days he had gone from perfect health to death.

This was a heartbreaking experience for all who knew him, but particularly for his father. This father was aware that his son was a most unusual young man, and the two of them, as well as being father and son, had been the dearest of friends. The father didn't know how he could carry on after sustaining the loss of this boy who had been so much the pride and love of his heart.

The night before the funeral, many people called at the mortuary, and one by one they tried to say those words that might bring comfort. But it seemed that the father couldn't be comforted. Finally there came a young man who was regarded by the other students as a social misfit. This boy, who was a loner, had very few friends. He had some problems that he hadn't brought upon himself but which limited him socially. As this awkward young man stood before the father he was not able to use any eloquent words whereby to offer any comfort.

He stood silently on that sacred ground and looked into the father's eyes. Then he began to sob. Amidst his sobs he was able to utter these words: "The only reason I ever came to school was because of your son. Every time I saw him in the hall he smiled, he stopped, and he talked to me. He made me feel that I was really somebody. He's the only one in the school who_ever did that. Now that he's gone, I don't know if I can even keep coming to school. He was the only friend I've ever had." These words pierced the very heart of the father, and he and the social misfit fell into one another's arms and wept together. To a greater degree than had been the case in many days, the father was comforted.

I Want to Be Your Friend

Allan K. Burgess and
Max H. Molgard

Tommy was one of the most difficult third-grade students the school had ever worked with. He was cross-eyed, dirty, and seemed to very seldom take a bath so he usually had very bad body odor. His gym shoes were tied together with string and his clothes were soiled and wrinkled. Many of the students taunted him and called him all kinds of names like "Stinky" and "Cross-eyes."

The teacher wondered what kind of parents would send Tommy to school this way, so she visited his house. It wasn't a house really; it was more like a large shack at the end of a dirt road. She found that Tommy's mother had died and that the father had a very low income and worked long hours. It was a very large family and there just wasn't enough money to go around. They had no hot water or electricity in their home, and while the teacher was there, an older sister was washing the family clothes in a tub filled with cold water in the center of the room. She didn't even have any soap to help get the clothes clean.

Tommy had no friends and he went to great lengths to try to show the other children that it didn't matter to him. Some days he would stand on his desk and tell the children in his class that he hated them before he would sit down. He refused to go outside for recess or lunch because this is when the other children were the most cruel to him.

The teacher tried everything she could think of to get Tommy and the other children to accept each other, but nothing seemed to work. Then she thought of William. William was one of the best third-grade students in the school and was in the same class as Tommy. The other children looked up to him, and he always seemed very kind and considerate. Maybe if she could somehow get Tommy and William to be friends, the rest of the class would fall into place.

She went to William and talked to him in private. She told him a little about Tommy and how much he needed a friend. She then asked him if he would be willing to try to be friends with Tommy, even if Tommy didn't want to be friends. He said that he would give it a try.

When it was time for recess, William went up to Tommy and asked him to go out and play with him. Tommy said that he didn't want to play with him and slugged William right in the nose. The blow knocked him to the floor. That would have been enough for most people, but William got up and said, "I don't care what you do to me; I'm going to be your friend." Tommy retorted that he didn't want a friend and knocked him to the floor again. William jumped up and approached Tommy the third time and, for the third time, hit the floor. But William would not quit—and the fourth time was different. When William said for the fourth time that he was going to be Tommy's friend, Tommy believed him, and friends they became.

From that time on, Tommy was a much happier person. He still had some problems and some learning disabilities, but once William became his friend, a few other children did also. It didn't take long for most of the children in the class to quit teasing Tommy and look for something more fun to do.

Love

RUTH G. ROTHE

Experts say that children must have
Tender loving care.
I, for one, think this is
Very true;
But some folks need reminding
Every now and then,
That middle aged and old folks
Need it too.

Stocking Caps

RICHARD M. SIDDOWAY

The seventh grade is a terrible time in one's life. The only thing that can make it worse is having to go to a new school where you know no one. Tom Stanley faced both challenges in his life when he moved to our community. It could have been easier, too, if Tom hadn't stuck out so clearly in a crowd. Although he had just turned twelve years of age, he looked about nine. He was the shortest and scrawniest seventh-grader in our school. His skin was so pale that it looked translucent, his eyes were a pale powder blue, and his hair was almost white. The only part of Tom Stanley that was twelve-year-old size was his nose, which hung like a hawk's beak on his face.

Warren Grimes, on the other hand, was the biggest kid in our class. There were rumors that Warren had been held back a year or two, but no one dared ask him about it. Warren was nearly six feet tall and over 250 pounds. In contrast to Tom Stanley, Warren was dark-complexioned and had an unruly thatch of black hair that he continually flipped out of his eyes with a jerk of his head. He constantly wore a red bandanna around his neck and dared anyone to touch it. It was his badge of honor. I knew of no one who liked Warren Grimes, nor did I know of anyone who dared cross him. Warren was the typical class bully.

The three of us shared first period together with Mr. Blake. Papa Blake, as we all called him behind his back, was our music teacher. He was near retirement, bald-headed and wizened, with rimless glasses and poorly fitting false teeth.

Mr. Blake had a unique seating chart. The first day of the semester, each of his students had to sing a solo for him. We all sang the same old spiritual, "Go Down, Moses, Way Down in

Egypt's Land." Mr. Blake listened intently and then separated us into sopranos, altos, and tenors. There were rarely any bass singers. The better your voice, the closer to the back of the room you sat. Frightened and embarrassed, I completed my solo and took my appointed front row seat in the alto section. Tom Stanley sat right across the aisle from me in the front seat of one of the soprano rows. Warren Grimes was the only bass.

I did not look forward to music class. I did not sing well and I had heard little of the music Papa Blake taught us to sing. There was one bright spot in first period, however. Gloria Chambers sat immediately behind me. I liked it when Papa Blake handed out sheets of music to the class because then I had license to turn around and look at Gloria while I passed the music to her. She had chestnut hair that hung to her shoulders, green eyes shrouded with long lashes, and the most beautiful pouting red lips I had ever seen. My heart beat with an unspoken love.

Not only did I sit next to Tom Stanley in class, but Mr. Blake assigned us lockers next to each other in the back of the upper hall. Tom had difficulty getting his combination lock to open. "Mr. Blake," he called out in his thin, reedy voice, "I can't get my lock to work."

Warren had opened his locker, three lockers further down the hall, and was standing nearly hidden behind the open door. "Mommy, Mommy, this is Tommy," he chanted. "Come and help your little guy before he starts to bawl and cry." And as if on command, tears started to roll down Tom's cheeks. He sniffed loudly and wiped his nose with the back of his hand before Mr. Blake reached him and helped him open his lock. Warren chuckled.

When lunchtime came I found myself standing a half-dozen people behind Tom in the lunch line. We pushed our cafeteria trays along the rails where the lunchroom workers handed us our plates of food. At the end of the rail Tom paused to pay for his lunch. As he balanced the tray in one hand and tried to put his change back in his pocket with the other, Warren Grimes bumped into him, sending the metal tray flying. "Watch out, you stupid little jerk," said Warren. Tom stood there mortified. The cashier turned at the sound of the tray hitting the floor.

"Don't just stand there," she said. "Pick it up." Tom knelt beside the tray and tried to retrieve what was left of his lunch. Both the spaghetti and the Jell-O had landed upside down. The roll and butter had skittered halfway across the cafeteria. His peanut butter cookie was nowhere to be seen. Only the carton of milk seemed salvageable. A custodian appeared with a bucket and mop and began cleaning up the mess. Tom, with tears running down his face, ran from the cafeteria.

Warren Grimes began to laugh and then to chant, "Tommy, Tommy, find your mommy." He retrieved the carton of milk from the floor and added it to his own tray of food. "Stupid little kid didn't even take his milk. Wouldn't want it to go to waste."

I did not have the same gym class as Tom and Warren, so I was not a witness to the "baseball incident," as Coach Simmons later called it. Apparently both boys were on the same team. Tom was told to play shortstop, and Warren elected to be pitcher. To be more accurate, they were playing softball, not baseball, but the result was the same. Tom and Warren's team was in the field, and a runner was on first base with two out. The batter hit a high fly into left field, and immediately the runner on first began running. The right fielder dropped the ball, retrieved it, and threw it toward the infield. Warren left the pitcher's mound and started running toward the incoming ball from left field. Tom did not move fast enough, and Warren knocked him to the ground, then tripped and fell on top of him. The ball bounced on by and the runner scored. Warren was infuriated. He began punching Tom in the face. Coach Simmons yelled at him, ran onto the field, and pulled Warren off of Tom.

"Stupid little jerk got in my way. I'll teach him," growled Warren.

"You go into my office and wait for me," commanded Coach Simmons as he spun Warren around and pointed him toward the school. "Are you all right?" he asked Tom as he knelt beside him.

Tears were flowing freely and mixing with the blood from Tom's nose. The rest of the class gathered around. Tom sobbed uncontrollably as he covered his bleeding nose with his hand. Coach Simmons helped him stagger to his feet. "Come with me," he said. "Let's get a cold towel on that. The rest of you boys go on in and shower."

The baseball incident became more graphic and violent with each retelling, but apparently there were no broken bones. Warren's parents were contacted and he was suspended from school for a few days. When he returned, he was apparently unrepentant, because the taunting of Tommy Stanley continued.

Each morning Tom waited until the last possible moment to scramble into first period, apparently hoping Warren Grimes would already be in his seat. Sometimes he was. Often he appeared immediately after Tom and walked down the aisle between us on the way to his back-row seat. Always he bumped into Tom's desk and sent his books and papers flying, or worse. On occasion he would turn to Gloria, ruffle her hair with his hand, and say, "Hi there, good-lookin'." This, of course, infuriated me, but I was too chicken to incur Warren's wrath.

One afternoon in the late autumn I walked out the back door of the school to head home. A large circle of kids had gathered on the lawn immediately to the west of the school. Curious, I joined them. There, in the middle of the circle, were Warren and Tom. Warren had grabbed Tom's arm and had it twisted behind him. "You stupid little jerk," hissed Warren. "Don't you never touch my neckerchief again. You got that?" Tom howled pitifully. "I said, you got that?" Warren spat out as he pushed Tom's arm a little higher. "And another thing. Don't you never talk to my girl again. I seen you sidlin' up to Gloria. You leave her alone. You got that, you stupid little jerk?" Warren threw Tom to the grass and stomped off. Tom remained a sobbing, sodden heap on the grass. The circle of students dispersed. I went to Tom's side and knelt down beside him.

"You all right?"

"Leave me alone," he sobbed. I shrugged my shoulders, stood, and walked home.

The next morning Gloria was in her seat when I took mine. Warren and Tom were nowhere to be seen. I swallowed hard, turned, and asked, "Gloria, are you really Warren's girlfriend?" I checked quickly to see if Warren had entered and seen me talking to her.

Gloria's green eyes blazed. "Of course not. He just thinks he can take anything he wants. Him and his stupid handkerchief."

I turned around, smiling.

Neither Warren nor Tom was there that day. Warren arrived the next day and tousled Gloria's hair on the way to his seat. Tom did not appear. In fact, it was three days before Tom showed up in class, and when he did he had a navy-blue stocking cap jammed on his head and pulled down over his ears. "Hey, Tom, how come you're wearing a cap?" I whispered. He just shrugged his shoulders and looked forlornly at his desk. Mr. Blake did not let us wear hats in class, but he seemed to ignore Tom's.

The next day he arrived wearing the same stocking cap. Something was obviously peculiar about this. In the middle of class Warren's hand shot up. "Mr. Blake, I gotta go to the bathroom."

Papa Blake peered at Warren. "Oh, all right, Warren, but hurry. We've got to get this music ready for the Christmas program."

Warren stood up from his seat and walked briskly down the aisle between Tom and me to the front of the room. As he passed Tom's desk, his hand flicked out and he pulled the stocking cap from Tom's head. The whole class gasped in unison. I heard Gloria behind me say, "Oh, no, poor Tom." Tom's head had been shaved completely bald and painted bright purple. Tom grabbed his cap from Warren and jammed it back on his head. Then he began to sob quietly. Warren sauntered out of the room.

Mr. Blake walked to Tom's desk and whispered something

in his ear. Tom arose, walked to the doorway, and looked warily into the hall, then left the room. Mr. Blake turned to the rest of us, who sat in shocked silence. "Class," he began, clearing his throat, "Tom has been diagnosed with a case of ringworm on his scalp. In order to treat it, the doctor shaves your head and paints it with something called methyl violet. It gets rid of the ringworm, but it won't wash off. It stays on your scalp for nearly a month. Tom has been given permission to wear a stocking cap until the color wears off." He seemed to be searching for the right words. "I don't believe Warren's actions were called for," he said at last. "I wish someone could do something to make Tom feel more accepted." He cleared his throat again and turned back to the music for the program.

Tom was not in school the next day. Gloria entered with a paper bag in her hand. She glowered at Warren as he walked past her on the way to his desk.

The next day Tom reappeared, stocking cap securely in place and eyes glued to the floor. He avoided looking at anyone as he took his front row seat. The bell rang and Mr. Blake rose to take roll. I heard the sound of a paper bag being extricated from Gloria's desk. And then a broad smile crossed Mr. Blake's face. I turned to see what he was smiling at. Gloria had pulled a stocking cap down on her head. She smiled at Tom.

The next day all of us, including Mr. Blake, wore stocking caps. More accurately, all of us but one, but then, maybe stocking caps and neckerchiefs don't go well together.

Forgiveness

Bridging the Ditch

LELAND E. ANDERSON

A wonderful Sunday School teacher once inspired my classmates and me, almost "stabbed" us all wide awake as would a divine surgeon, with the necessity of living daily in a manner pleasing to the Lord. He made us feel that our sacred scriptures could always be a point of reference that would lead us to God's celestial kingdom. A powerful testimony of this came to me as a result of an experience in my daily life, an experience that was truly a crossroads to me.

In my home town was a large pea factory. Peas were never picked in the patch; they were cut in the vine like hay, and loaded—green vines and all—on a hay wagon. A relatively small forkful could seem like a load of lead.

One morning as I was mowing some alfalfa, the fieldman from the factory came to me and said, "Your pea patch is ready right now to be harvested." This is a crucial point—a few hours of too much sunshine turns peas in a pod from first-class to hard tack. Much value of the crop is lost if it is not cut on time.

I moved my team and hay-cutting equipment to the five-acre pea patch and in a short time had cut all the hayrack would hold; in fact, it was all my small team could pull. With some effort and the help of a switch, I managed to get the team to pull the load to the hardened field road. Then we proceeded toward the factory a mile away. However, I had forgotten all about the old field ditch, full of water, which my team had to cross. Would I ever make it?

I soon discovered the answer. Approaching the ditch, I first gave the team a much-needed rest. Then, with positive urging, they shot across the ditch—but the front wheels hit the mud and sank up to the hub!

The only solution was for me to unload all the peas on the ground, pull the empty wagon across, and then proceed to carry the peas and replace them upon the wagon. The very thought made me tired. If only another team and wagon would appear on the scene—maybe two teams could pull me out!

Then up the road I could see an outfit coming in my direction. Help was in sight. As the wagon came closer, however, my heart sank. It was my neighbor who lived down the road and who did not help anyone. He didn't have to—he was rich in worldly goods.

As he pulled up beside me, he stopped his outfit and smilingly said, "So, you're stuck, are you, Lee?" I was surprised he knew my name. He had never talked to me before. I replied that my load was too big for my small team. His smile grew larger as he said, "Well, good luck to you," and away he went down the lane.

Never was I so angry! What I called him cannot be printed—I even spoke in Danish so my team couldn't understand! For the moment I reappraised the law of Moses. I looked up into the sky and said, "Oh, Father, give me the chance to meet him on the desert sometime, choking for a good drink of water. Let me have a barrel of water in my truck so I can pour it out onto the sand and tell him to scratch."

Somehow I managed to get to the factory. I succeeded in getting all of my peas harvested in time, and though my feelings were still on edge they had mellowed somewhat.

Evil seldom requires a down payment; it's like installment buying. My hope—and my day—finally arrived. A few days later, while proceeding to my farm, as I approached this roadblock to my farming efforts, the ditch, I nearly choked with happiness. I found my unobliging neighbor stuck in the same ditch with a load of peas!

Before I reached the scene of trouble, like a bolt of lightning my Sunday School teacher's lesson on retaliation came to my mind. I tried to unload the thought, but it was deeply entrenched in my soul. Our Savior said, "And whosoever shall compel thee to go a mile, go with him twain." (Matthew 5:41.)

Now or never was my life to be molded by love or hatred. The Lord had said, "Agree with thine adversary quickly, whiles thou art in the way with him." (Matthew 5:25.) I did! I kicked the adversary off the wagon.

As I pulled up beside my brother, I stopped and repeated to him his own words: "So you're stuck, are you, brother?" I hoped he would learn from this new experience the lesson that Cain learned in the garden, that there is no such thing as liberty without law.

My neighbor responded that he could not proceed without help. I did not wait longer. I jumped off my wagon, took from it a long chain, and secured it properly onto the end of his wagon tongue. Then the two teams put their shoulders to the wheel and in short order they were all standing on dry ground.

In deep embarrassment, my neighbor said, "Thanks, Lee. I appreciate your kindness." Then he added, "How much do I owe you?"

My reply was not altogether honest. "I enjoyed helping you out of that ditch," I said.

We both went on our way rejoicing. I could hardly hold my team—they seemed to want to trot. And I caught myself whistling and singing, "Come, Come, Ye Saints."

A couple of days later I found a new bridge over the ditch. I smiled as I learned who had obliged all the north field farmers with this needed contribution.

Two weeks later, while cutting more hay one day, I noticed a man coming down through my field. It was my neighbor. "Let your team have a break, while we settle the problems of the world," he said. So we visited for a few minutes. Then, as he started to leave, he looked squarely at me and, in halting phrases, apologized for leaving me in the ditch.

I have often wondered just which one of us was the unneighborly one. When had I ever volunteered to him any kindness? The injured one may well be the one at times who seeks confrontation and better understanding. We both learned a valuable lesson that day.

"To Show Them That Love Is Greater"

CORRIE TEN BOOM

Editor's Note: Dutch sisters Corrie and Betsie ten Boom were sent to a concentration camp for assisting Jews during the Nazis' onslaught in Holland. Both sisters, well into their fifties when they arrived in Ravensbruck, learned invaluable lessons in that horrible death camp. The following is an example of their courage and ability to forgive in the midst of terrible oppression.

Though Betsie was now spared heavy outdoor labor, she still had to stand the twice-daily roll call. As December temperatures fell, they became true endurance tests and many did not survive. One dark morning when ice was forming a halo around each street lamp, a feeble-minded girl two rows ahead of us suddenly soiled herself. A guard rushed at her, swinging her thick leather crop while the girl shrieked in pain and terror. It was always more terrible when one of these innocent ones was beaten. Still the Aufseherin continued to whip her. It was the guard we had nicknamed "The Snake" because of the shiny dress she wore. I could see it now beneath her long wool cape, glittering in the light of the lamp as she raised her arm. I was grateful when the screaming girl at last lay still on the cinder street.

"Betsie," I whispered when The Snake was far enough away, "what can we do for these people? Afterward I mean. Can't we make a home for them and care for them and love them?"

"Corrie, I pray every day that we will be allowed to do this! To show them that love is greater!"

And it wasn't until I was gathering twigs later in the morning that I realized that I had been thinking of the feeble-minded, and Betsie of their persecutors.

$\mathcal{B}$etter Than Revenge

GLENN HAMPTON

Editor's Note: The story of Glenn Hampton's remarkable ability to forgive began on February 10, 1918, when four officers of the law—Glenn's father being one of them—journeyed to the mountains of Southern Arizona to enforce the draft law on the Powers boys, who had failed to register. Three of the four officers were killed that cold morning, leaving three young widows and nineteen orphaned children.

It happened on the tenth of February, 1918, high in the fastnesses of the Galiuro Mountains in southern Arizona. It was a cold, grey dawn, sky overcast, snow gently falling, when Father was shot down from behind. Two other law officers also lost their lives in the withering blast that emitted forth from the little log-cabin fortress in which the draft evaders had taken refuge.

After a cautious ten or fifteen minutes waiting, they came outside to view the remains of their grisly work. Having satisfied themselves that they had killed the entire party, they bore their father, who had received a mortal wound, into a nearby tunnel, covered him with an old blanket, sent word to a nearby rancher to look after him, saddled their horses and headed south. Destination—Old Mexico!

There followed one of the greatest man-hunts in the southwest history. The draft evaders were finally run down and caught near the Mexican border. They were tried and found guilty of murder, for which they received sentences of life imprisonment.

As a young boy in my early teens, there grew in my heart a bitterness and a hatred toward the confessed slayer of my Father, for Tom Powers had admitted killing my Dad.

The years swept by, I grew up, but still that heavy feeling stayed inside me. High school ended, and then I received a call to go to the Eastern States Mission. There my knowledge and testimony of the gospel grew rapidly, as all of my time was spent studying and preaching it. One day while reading the New Testament, I came to Matthew, fifth chapter, verses 43 to 45, wherein Jesus said:

"Ye have heard that it hath been said, Thou shalt love thy neighbour and hate thine enemy. But I say unto you, Love your enemies, bless them that curse you, do good to them that hate you, and pray for them that despitefully use you and persecute you; that ye may be the children of your Father which is in heaven. . . ."

Here it was, the words of the Savior saying we should forgive. This applied to me. I read those verses again and again and it still meant forgiveness. Not very long after this, I found in the 64th section of the Doctrine and Covenants, verses 9 and 10, more of the Savior's words:

"Wherefore, I say unto you, that ye ought to forgive one another; for he that forgiveth not his brother his trespasses standeth condemned before the Lord; for there remaineth in him the greater sin. I, the Lord, will forgive whom I will forgive, but of you it is required to forgive all men."

And then there were these timely words of President John Taylor:

"Forgiveness is in advance of Justice where repentance is concerned."

I didn't know whether or not Tom Powers had repented but I did know now that I had an appointment to make after I returned home, and I resolved before I left the mission field to do just that.

After returning home, I met and married a fine Latter-day Saint girl, and the Lord blessed our home with five lovely children. The years were passing rapidly and the Lord had been good to us, yet guilt arose within me every time I thought of the appointment I had not kept.

A few years ago, just shortly before Christmas, a season when the love of Christ abounds and the spirit of giving and forgiving gets inside of us, my wife and I were in Phoenix on a short trip. Having concluded our business in the middle of the second afternoon, we started home. As we rode along, I expressed the desire to detour and return home via Florence, for that is where the state prison is located. My wife readily assented.

It was after visiting hours when we arrived but I went on inside and asked for the warden. I was directed to his office.

After I had introduced myself and expressed a desire to meet and talk to Tom Powers, a puzzled expression came over the warden's face, but after only a slight hesitation, he said, "I'm sure that can be arranged." Whereupon he dispatched a guard down into the compound who soon returned with Tom. We were introduced, and led into the parole room where we had a long talk. We went back to that cold, gray February morning thirty years before, re-enacting that whole terrible tragedy. We talked for perhaps an hour and a half. Finally, I said, "Tom, you made a mistake for which you owe a debt to society for which I feel you must continue to pay, just the same as I must continue to pay the price for having been reared without a father."

Then I stood and extended my hand. He stood and took it.

I continued, "With all my heart, I forgive you for this awful thing that has come into our lives."

He bowed his head and I left him there. I don't know how he felt then, and I don't know how he feels now, but my witness to you is that it is a glorious thing when bitterness and hatred go out of your heart and forgiveness comes in.

I thanked the warden for his kindness, and as I walked out the door and down that long flight of steps I knew that forgiveness was better than revenge, for I had experienced it. .

As we drove toward home in the gathering twilight, a sweet and peaceful calm came over me. Out of pure gratitude I placed my arm around my wife, who understood, for I know that we had now found a broader, richer and more abundant life.

Love Your Enemies

HARRY EMERSON FOSDICK

In the course of the Armenian atrocities a young woman and her brother were pursued down the street by a Turkish soldier, cornered in an angle of the wall, and the brother was slain before his sister's eyes. She dodged down an alley, leaped a wall, and escaped. Later, being a nurse, she was forced by the Turkish authorities to work in the military hospital. Into her ward was brought, one day, the same Turkish soldier who had slain her brother. He was very ill. A slight inattention would insure his death. The young woman, now safe in America, confesses to the bitter struggle that took place in her mind. The old

Adam cried, "Vengeance"; the new Christ cried, "Love." And, equally to the man's good and to her own, the better side of her conquered, and she nursed him as carefully as any other patient in the ward. The recognition had been mutual and one day, unable longer to restrain his curiosity, the Turk asked his nurse why she had not let him die, and when she replied, "I am a follower of him who said 'Love your enemies and do them good,'" he was silent for a long time. At last he spoke: "I never knew that there was such a religion. If that is your religion tell me more about it, for I want it."

True Brotherhood

Richard M. Siddoway

Sean was two and a half years old when Kelly was born. But by the time Kelly was eight years old, they looked like twins. It wasn't so much that Sean was short as it was that Kelly was tall for his age. Sean was quite relieved when he entered junior high and no longer attended the same school as his fifth-grade brother.

For two blissful years none of his teachers asked him if Kelly was his twin. It helped further that Sean's junior high school began an hour earlier than Kelly's school, so the two of them didn't even walk to school together.

Of course, the family was a different matter. According to Sean, their Aunt Rhoda could be counted on to go through the same ritual every time she visited. "You two boys stand back to back," she'd warble. "Let's see if Kelly has caught up to Sean."

The two of them would accordingly stand back to back, and their Aunt Rhoda would place her hand on top of their heads. "Not yet, Kelly, not yet. Sean still has you by half an inch."

The ritual never changed until the summer before Kelly entered junior high. "Stand back to back," Aunt Rhoda commanded. "Well, Kelly baby, I do believe you're taller than your big brother."

During the school year Kelly continued his growth spurt so that by the end of the year he was nearly an inch taller than Sean. Sean became depressed. The two brothers had always bickered with each other, but now it increased. Sean was jealous. Solace was but a summer away; then he'd attend high school and get away from his pesky little . . . no, make that his pesky younger brother.

I'd known the family for nearly twenty years. I'd watched the two boys grow up and had been as unthinking as anyone else when I commented on their relative sizes. That fall when Sean entered high school he ended up in my biology class. He had grown to a respectable height just shy of six feet. His eighth-grade brother, however, was nearly three inches taller. The only part of Sean that had kept up with Kelly's growth was his feet. Both boys wore size twelve shoes.

When basketball season began I was pleased to see Sean on the sophomore team. He was not a brilliant player, but he was steady. He could handle the ball well, and although he rarely took a shot, his assists were responsible for a number of baskets. Although my assignment was to videotape the varsity games for the basketball coach, I often arrived early enough to watch the sophomore games. They finished the season with a winning record. By the end of the year Sean had grown another half inch and seemed to have reached his full height.

That same year Kelly was the star of the eighth-grade team. Not only was he taller than any player on the opposing teams, he was well coordinated and had a devastating jump shot. He intimidated the other teams with his size and ability. Our local paper ran a story about Kelly on the front page of the sports section. The local sports reporter, who is known to exaggerate on occasion, suggested that Kelly was at least college material, if not a potential NBA first-round draft choice. Sean was jealous. Kelly's ego was inflated. They barely had a kind word to say to each other.

The next year didn't improve the situation. Sean tried out for the basketball team and made it, but as a junior he spent most of the time on the bench. Our team had a winning record, but only in the final minute of a game that was clearly out of reach did Sean have an opportunity to play. When the team went to the state tournament, Sean's total playing time in four games was forty-one seconds. He attempted one basket, which he missed. He did have an assist during his brief time on the court.

Kelly's ninth-grade team went undefeated. Kelly scored twenty-two points and blocked six shots in the district championship game. He was the hero of the school. The local newspaper ran a picture on the front page of him making a short hook shot. "An Irresistible Force," blared the headline. He was presented with a framed photograph of himself at a school assembly where he was named most valuable player, as well as athlete of the week by the newspaper.

Kelly hung the photograph on the wall opposite the front door of their home, so that anyone entering would see it. He placed his most-valuable-player trophy on the table beneath the photograph. Sean began using the back door so he wouldn't have to see Kelly's shrine. He was extremely jealous. The two brothers rarely spoke to each other, and when they did, acid hung in the air between them.

Sean became a starter on the basketball team during his senior year. He was slightly over six feet, and a good ball handler. He valued his starting position. Kelly began the preseason as the center on the sophomore team. With one preseason game to go, Kelly appeared on the bench with the varsity team. Still Sean was not worried. The team had a senior center who was an inch taller than his brother, and a good player. The chance that Kelly would get into a game seemed slim. In fact, it seemed to Sean that he'd be on the court playing and his brother would have to sit on the bench watching. It felt good.

As the season progressed, it was obvious that our team was the team to beat. Sean had played in every game. He was averaging just over four points and nearly eight assists per game. Kelly had played a few minutes in several of the games. It was clear he was able to take the ball to the hoop, but the senior center had more experience. With one game to go in the regular season, our team had won every game but one. For our final game we were to play the only team that had beaten us. Since our opponent had lost one game as well, the team that won the contest would enter the state tournament as the first-place team from our region.

The game was played in our gymnasium, but there was little home court advantage since the opposing team brought equally as many fans. We were seated on the south, they on the north. The place was packed, the noise level deafening.

At the end of the first quarter the two teams had battled to a tie—eighteen points each. At halftime our home team was leading by three points. Both teams had played their starting five for the entire half. Ten totally fatigued young men went to the locker rooms with their teammates.

Both teams slowed down the pace during the third quarter. Each tried to move the ball around to get high percentage shots. The teams traded baskets back and forth, and at the end of the third quarter we led by a single point.

"We're going to do it, men," the coach encouraged. "Sean, you're doing a great job. Just keep feeding that ball to the open man." Sean nodded his agreement. The horn blew and the fourth quarter began.

As the ball was thrown in to start the quarter, an opposing player stole it and raced the length of the court for a lay-up. The fans in the north bleachers screamed their approval. Sean calmly brought the ball down the court. He dribbled the ball toward the right angle of the court. The center broke loose from his man, took three steps from the right side of the lane to the left, and leapt in the air. Sean fired the ball to him and he drilled the ball through the hoop. Now the fans in the south bleachers erupted in screams.

Down the court they raced. The opposing forward shot a short jumper that bounced straight up off the rim. Both centers leapt for the rebound and crashed into each other, falling to the floor. No whistle blew. The ball bounced out of bounds. There was a collective "Ooh" from the crowd. The opposing center got back on his feet and, in a gesture of sportsmanship, reached his hand down to our center. Our player tried to stand, but it was obvious he had sprained his left ankle. Time-out was called, and he was helped from the court. The team doctor examined his ankle and put an ice pack on it. The doctor looked at the coach and shook his head. A moan of dismay went through the south bleachers.

Our coach looked down the row of chairs and beckoned to Kelly. Sean felt a knot in the pit of his stomach. "Men," said the coach, "we can still do it. We're up by a point, and we all know this is not a one-man team. Now, get in there and let's put this one away."

Kelly checked in at the scorekeeper's table and entered the game. The other team threw in the ball. Carefully they worked it around the perimeter until their center pivoted free. The ball was fired into him and he turned to shoot. As the ball left his hand, Kelly swatted it away from the basket. The crowd roared. Sean fought for the ball and came away with it. He drove down the court to the top of the key. He was in the clear. He launched a shot toward the basket. The ball bounced off the back of the rim, and at that moment Kelly arrived in full stride, grabbed the rebound, jumped, and put the ball in the basket. We were ahead by three points.

Kelly sprinted down the court and positioned himself at the left side of the lane just in time to see their point guard shoot a jumper from near the top of the key. The ball swished through the net. He grabbed the ball, stepped out of bounds, and saw his brother waiting for the ball. A man was just behind him ready to steal the ball. The other guard was further down the court. Kelly threw the ball to him.

Sean was fuming. His brother wouldn't even throw him the ball! Down the court they came. The ball was thrown to Sean.

His brother cut toward the basket. For one brief moment Sean hesitated, then he threw the ball to his younger brother, who laid the ball up for two points. The game continued. The lead switched back and forth.

They were down by one point with sixty-three seconds left in the game when the coach called a time-out, "Men," he said, "we've got one minute to prove ourselves." The boys listened intently. "Kelly, you've done a great job in the center. If it weren't for you we wouldn't still be in this game."

The little boy in Sean wanted to call out, *What about me? I've been getting him the ball so he could score. How great do you think he'd be without the rest of us?* But in one maturing moment of truth, he realized the coach was right. Without his younger brother's efforts, they would not be winning this game.

The coach outlined the play he wanted run and they were about to go back on the court, when Sean noticed the sole of Kelly's right shoe. It was beginning to peel off from the toe of the shoe. As they walked back on the court, Sean could see the first inch or so of Kelly's sole flip-flopping loose.

Sean took the inbound pass and began to set up the play. Seconds ticked off the clock until finally he was able to thread a pass to the forward, who spun around and launched a shot at the basket. The ball banged off the side of the rim. Kelly leapt for the rebound, grabbed it, came down, and went back up to stuff the ball home. He came back down with his foot sticking half out of his shoe. He tried to run down the court, but his shoe wouldn't let him. The other team took advantage of the situation and regained the lead with sixteen seconds left. As Kelly struggled to get his foot and shoe put back together, his older brother brought the ball down the court. He looked back at Kelly, who was sitting on the floor working with his shoe. Suddenly Sean let out a cry and fell to the floor. Protecting the ball, he signaled a time-out and then grabbed his leg and began massaging it as he rolled around on the floor in obvious agony. The team doctor ran onto the court for the second time that night. He and the coach picked up Sean and carried him to his seat.

The team gathered around while the doctor massaged Sean's

right calf. The doctor pulled off Sean's shoe and pushed his toes back toward his shin while he manipulated the calf muscles. Sean moaned in obvious pain. He reached down, retrieved his shoe, and handed it to Kelly. "Put it on," he said through clenched teeth. "At least one of us ought to be in the game." Kelly pulled off his damaged shoe and laced on Sean's.

The whistle blew and the game continued. Twelve seconds showed on the clock. We were down by one point. Ten seconds later, Sean's replacement threw the ball to Kelly, who banked in the winning shot. A desperation court-long shot by our opponents fell short.

If I had not videotaped the game, I probably would have missed the miraculous healing of Sean's muscle spasm. But on instant replay he's there with the rest of the team, leaping up and down, wearing a single shoe.

$\mathscr{B}$ut He That Loseth His Life . . .

NAME WITHHELD

$\mathbf{O}$ne year into my mission I was assigned, as a district leader, to be the companion of an elder who had been in the mission field four or five months longer than I had. We had both served as senior companions and he seemed somewhat offended that I was to be not only his companion, but also the district leader, which effectively made me his senior companion. It was an awkward situation, and I'm sure it was quite as uncomfortable for him as it was for me. As we began to work together there were a few stumbling blocks, but most of our time together was spent working harmoniously.

One day we were teaching the gospel to a family who had been referred to us by a member of our branch. I had presented the first discussion and had made an appointment to return to teach them the second. After we left their home, my companion said that he just didn't think the family was ready and that we were wasting our time teaching them. I answered that they were the best teaching situation we had at the time and that we had better spend our time working with them.

As we proceeded through the discussions with that family my companion took a passive role in the conversion process. Instead of taking turns teaching the lesson on each visit, he withdrew his participation somewhat, requiring me to give all the discussions and to take the lead in teaching the family. As we continued to teach them they became more and more receptive until, after several weeks, they set a date to be baptized.

The day of the baptism came. That morning, as we were getting ready to leave, I couldn't find the forms we had filled out during the baptismal interviews. I had just seen them a few days before and I knew that we had them, but now they were missing. I asked my companion if he knew where they were and he said that they were in his briefcase. I thought that that was curious, but as we prayed before leaving the apartment it became evident to me that he was planning to take over the final details of the baptism. In other words, after contributing almost nothing to the process, or to the family, he was going to step in and take over some of the most rewarding aspects of the work.

As it dawned on me what was happening I could see the potential for ruining the baptismal day of this family if we were to argue or fight over who was to conduct the interviews and who was to perform the baptisms. I searched my mind and found comfort in the thought that the most important thing was the welfare of the family—that this day should really become a day that they would remember forever. It should be a time for being touched again by the witness of the Spirit, and I knew that the Spirit could not be present when two missionaries were being influenced by the spirit of contention. I did not want to detract from the converts' experience in any way, so I resolved, absolutely, to exert my faith in their behalf so that it would be their special day.

I remember riding along the beach in the open streetcar to the family's home and praying that they would feel the Holy Ghost touch them and testify to them, again, that this was truly the restored gospel. As I did so I felt a sweet confirmation of the Spirit that it would be a wonderful day for them and, in addition, I felt a feeling of personal contentment that I perceived was designed particularly for me. It removed from my soul any bitterness or disappointment at the course my companion had chosen. I did not feel what I had expected to feel. I was at peace. In fact, the influence of the Spirit was so sweet for me that I remember almost arguing with the Lord that what I had been asking was a witness for them, not for me. But he had recognized that two teaching opportunities existed simultaneously—a wonderful family and a young elder. He responded to both.

As we arrived in the family's home I continued that prayer, and when my companion pulled out the paperwork and began the interviews it slowly became evident to them that he would be the one to perform the baptisms that day. I was very supportive of the procedure, and as they looked my way I confirmed that my companion would be doing the baptisms and smiled in the most positive way I knew how. The baptismal interviews proceeded successfully, as did the baptisms. The day turned out to be all that I had prayed for and was, in fact, one that they can look back on as a spiritual milestone.

Now, twenty-seven years later, it is a source of real joy to know that the gospel has become precious to them. Their lives in the intervening years have been exemplary. I thank my Heavenly Father for having had the opportunity of working with this faithful family.

As I reflect back on that day and its events I hold no animosity toward a companion who engaged in some actions that were out of character for him. Instead, I remember that day as one in which we had one of our finest baptisms and in which I felt a deeper understanding of the principle reason why I was a missionary—not to register baptisms in my name, but to lead families to the Savior.

$\mathcal{A}$ Man of God

Elaine Cannon

Geroge Albert Smith was a young Utah National Guardsman when he learned the value of reconciliation. He was being considered for some kind of special leadership assignment or personal award, when a man he thought was his friend started damaging rumors about him.

George lost the recognition because of this cruel act. He felt he was entitled to it and that he had been cheated out of it. His heart filled with hurt and anger toward his former friend. His life became miserable. The more he thought about the disappointing situation, the more it ballooned in importance and destroyed his peace.

His bitterness escalated to the point where he felt uncomfortable taking the sacrament of the Lord's Supper. He began to pray about it. He desired some kind of revenge, but he was a disciple of Christ and knew that such action was not in keeping with such high ideals. Although he did nothing overtly to destroy the guilty man, the hurt still rankled his soul. Time passed, and George finally grasped the perspective that the incident hadn't seemed to affect his former friend. He, George Albert Smith, was wronging only himself with the burden of hate he carried.

Reconciliation was the only answer. Get it off his chest and be done with it. Life was about more than this.

He went to the place of business of the man who had spread the damaging falsehoods. When the man saw George Albert coming, he automatically raised his arm in a kind of mock shield over his face. He thought he was in for a beating.

George Albert had prepared himself for the occasion through fervent prayer. By the time he had courageously made the attempt to confront his enemy, he was mollified and full of the Spirit. His voice was gentle and his manner humble. He considered himself at fault for giving in to hate and anger. He expressed this to his friend, who lowered his arm, bowed his head, and listened quietly as George Albert said, "I want you to forgive me for the anger I have felt in these past weeks, for the way I have been hating."

"George Albert, you have no need for forgiveness. It is I who need forgiveness from you."

Because of Smith's spiritual maturity and his willingness to reconcile past problems in favor of peace, the enemy was subdued. Friendship was possible again.

Of such is a man of God made.

$\mathcal{S}$ilence

NEAL A. MAXWELL

I 've learned that silence can be productive, even though it makes us very anxious. A fine colleague and friend called my office shortly after I had been sustained as a General Authority to ask for an appointment. I was out, but happily my secretary scheduled an appointment, and it was for more than a mere ten minutes. The friend came. I greeted him warmly, but, contrary to my usual style, I stayed mostly silent. His eyes brimmed with tears as finally he said that, as he had listened to conference, he knew he needed to come and set things right. I resisted the impulse to intervene reassuringly, since I knew of nothing that was wrong. He then continued, saying that he was becoming active in the Church again and knew he needed to repair certain relationships. Happily, again I resisted stemming his flow of feeling. With courage and tenderness, he indicated that at times he had said things about me that were untrue and unkind. He wanted to seek my forgiveness. Only then did I respond by telling him of my regard for him and my unawareness of and unconcern over what he had reportedly said. Most importantly, I told him of my love and admiration and forgiveness. We embraced. I expressed then my admiration also for his courage and for his manhood. He then said how difficult it had been to come that day and how he had almost called to cancel the appointment. We spoke together of the wisdom contained in Matthew 18:15 and Jesus' counsel therein as to what we should do when there are impasses in human relationships: "Moreover if thy brother shall trespass against thee, go and tell him his fault between thee and him alone: if he shall hear thee, thou hast gained thy brother." I love that man and respect him for taking the initiative, since I had been unaware of the matter. He is fully and effectively active in the kingdom today. He needed to say what he said more than I needed to hear it, but I am so grateful I did not rush in to fill the silence that morning in the lesson he taught me so well.

Roses Are Red

Richard M. Siddoway

Today is December 23. It is on this day each year that I do penance for an act I committed in 1947, when I was seven years old. I was in the third grade at Emerson School and had been blessed with a marvelous teacher named Miss Heacock. She was not much taller than I, and had dark red hair and smiling green eyes. I credit her with any love I have for classical music, because she spent part of every Thursday morning introducing us to the lives of the great composers and playing recordings of music by Beethoven, Brahms, Bach, and other great musicians. I loved the school because of the influence of this wonderful woman.

As Christmas approached we made decorations for our schoolroom. Miles of red and green paper strips were pasted into interlocking loops to form paper chains as we listened to Handel's *Messiah*. Pictures of Santa Claus were drawn and painted with water colors. Stained-glass windows were approximated as Miss Heacock ironed our crayon drawings between pieces of scrap paper. A Christmas tree was placed in one front corner of the room, and the odor of pine replaced the particularly pungent aroma of oil that arose from the decades-old hardwood floors of our classroom. It was then that Miss Heacock announced we were to have a Christmas party on the day we were released for Christmas vacation. We were all excited.

Fate had blessed us with a peculiar situation that year. There were exactly as many girls as boys in our class. Miss Heacock decided, perhaps in an attempt to introduce us to the social graces, that each of us would purchase a gift for another student in the room. Each boy would supply a gift for a girl and vice versa. The gifts were to cost no more than twenty-five cents. There have been moments in my life when I have known exactly what was going to happen. I claim no great gift of prophecy, but, nevertheless, I have known. As Miss Heacock began walking down the aisles, a box of boys' names in one hand, one with girls' names in the other, I knew the name I'd draw would be Violet's.

Violet was a sorry little girl who had been placed in our class that year. She was very plain and did little to help her looks. Her hair was rarely combed, she wore the same dress every day, and worst of all, she wet the bed and rarely bathed. Violet sat in the back corner of the room, partially because she chose to sit there, but also because the rest of us had moved away from her. When the room warmed up, the aroma of Violet mixed with the perfume of floor oil and became almost overpowering. Seven- and eight-year-old children can be cruel, very cruel. Violet had been the target of most of our cruelty during the school year.

Miss Heacock approached my desk with the box of girls' names. I reached into the box, shuffled the names around, and finally withdrew the folded scrap of paper. I placed it before me on my desk. My finger trembled as I unfolded it. There it was, as I knew it would be: "Violet." I quickly wadded up the paper and shoved it into my pants pocket. The bell rang for recess.

"Who'd you get?" asked my best friend, Allen.

I panicked. I couldn't let anyone know I'd gotten Violet. "We're supposed to keep it secret."

"Sure, but you can tell *me*," Allen probed. "I'll tell you who I got. Just between us, okay?"

"Miss Heacock said to keep it secret." My voice squeaked a little.

Suddenly Allen smiled. Earlier in the year I had made the mistake of telling him I thought one of the girls in our class, Margo of the honey-colored hair, was pretty. I had endured considerable abuse since that disclosure. "I'll bet you got Margo's name. That's why you won't tell. You got Margo!" Immediately he was running around the playground shouting that I'd gotten Margo's name. So much for Allen's ability to keep a secret.

I slunk back into the school, face aflame. The rest of that Friday crawled by. Finally the last bell rang. As I was pulling on my galoshes I felt a hand on my shoulder. "Is something wrong?" I looked up into Miss Heacock's emerald eyes. "You seemed awfully quiet this afternoon."

"I'm okay," I stammered. My mind had been struggling with the Violet problem all afternoon. I had reached a possible solution; I wouldn't get Violet anything. Since we were maintaining secrecy, no one would know. "Maybe," I said, "I won't be able to get a present. My father makes me earn all my spending money," I lied, "and I might not have a quarter to buy a present."

A look of concern came over Miss Heacock's face. "If you can't afford a quarter, I'll give you one. It will be our little secret."

I trudged home through the snow. No other brilliant escapes from the situation entered my mind. Christmas was the following Thursday, and the party would be on Tuesday. I had only three days to find a way out of my misery. Perhaps I could become sick, but that path was fraught with peril, since my mother made us stay in bed all day when we were sick, and I might be in bed Christmas Day if she suspected I was really not sick. At last I reached home.

The house smelled wonderful. I could tell my mother had been baking bread. I hurried to the kitchen in hopes of melting gobs of butter on a slice of warm bread. My mother greeted me. "Miss Heacock phoned. I'm sure your father and I can come up with a quarter for a Christmas present." My heart sank into my galoshes. Now there was no way out.

Saturday morning it was snowing. My mother exulted about a white Christmas while I pulled on my snowsuit and galoshes and prepared for the four-block trek to the Economy Drug Store. My mother gave me a quarter and a dime "just in case" and sent me off to do my Christmas shopping. I took time to investigate everything along the way, prolonging the inevitable as long as possible.

Since the previous evening, I had been contemplating what to buy for Violet. Nothing seemed really appropriate. As I wandered up and down the aisles of the Economy Drug, galoshes squeaking mournfully, I discovered my choices were somewhat narrowed by the twenty-five cent limit. I considered purchasing five nickel candy bars but discarded that idea, since Violet probably liked candy bars. As I reached the end of the counter, I saw the gift, and a terrible plan exploded full-blown in my mind. Not only did I see the gift, but I knew how I would present it to Violet. There on the shelf were small, crown-shaped bottles of cologne. I selected one from the display and twisted off the lid. Years later when I read novels that used the phrase "she reeked of cheap perfume," my mind always flashed back to the first whiff of cologne from that bottle in the Economy Drug. It had only one redeeming feature. It cost a quarter.

I sloshed back home with my purchase. Thankfully, my mother did not sniff the cologne. She merely commented on how lovely the little bottle was. She helped me find a box and wrap my gift. I went to my room, found a pencil and paper, and wrote the following poem:

> *Roses are red,*
> *Violets are blue,*
> *Put this stuff on*
> *So we can stand you.*

I did not sign it. I sealed it in an envelope and taped it to the gift.

Monday morning I left for school earlier than usual. When I arrived I went to my classroom. The door was open, but Miss Heacock was not in her room. Quickly and furtively I placed the gift under the Christmas tree. So far so good.

By the time the school bell rang, Miss Heacock was playing Christmas carols on the phonograph, and more and more gifts were being placed under the tree. We became more excited about tomorrow's Christmas party as the day wore on. Miss Heacock carefully looked at each gift and checked off names in her roll book.

On Tuesday our party was preceded by a semiannual desk clean out. At last all of the papers had been removed, crayon boxes lined up neatly, and pencils sharpened and put away. It was time for the party!

We drank punch from paper cups and ate cookies and candy canes, and then it was time to distribute gifts. As we sat in our seats Miss Heacock selected a present from beneath the tree and called out, "Sandra." Sandra, somewhat embarrassed, walked to the front of the room and took her present back to her desk. She was unsure whether she should open it or not. "You may open it, Sandra," said Miss Heacock.

Several more presents were distributed before Miss Heacock called out, "Violet." Violet walked slowly to the front of the room. Miss Heacock extended her hand and delivered my gift. Violet, eyes glistening, walked back to her seat. I shifted in my seat so I could see her reaction. She placed the unopened gift on her desk and opened the envelope. Suddenly she began to quiver; a tear formed in the corner of her eye and ran down her cheek. Violet began to sob. She grabbed her present and ran from the room. Miss Heacock, reaching for a gift, did not see her go.

The enormity of what I had done sank home. Tears filled my eyes. There have been moments in my life when I wished I could back up ten minutes and correct errors I had made. This was one of those moments. I am sure my name was eventually called. I am sure I was given a gift. I remember nothing of this. I merely wallowed in guilt. Finally the party ended, and I walked home.

As Christmas vacation came to an end I began to realize I would have to face Violet when I went back to school. Even though I had not signed my name, I was certain she had figured out who had written that terrible poem. How could I face her? But like it or not, school began again. It began without Violet. Her seat was empty. It was empty the next day and the next. Violet had moved.

Twelve years passed. I entered a classroom at the University of Utah and took my seat. The professor began to call the roll. "Violet," he called. The girl in the seat directly behind mine answered, "Here." My blood ran cold. As discreetly as possible I turned and looked at her. She had matured, she had changed from an ugly duckling into a swan, but there was no doubt it was Violet.

When class ended I turned to her. "Violet," I said, "I don't know if you remember me. We were in the same class in third grade at Emerson School."

She looked at me, and her forehead wrinkled. "I'm sorry, I really don't remember your name. I was only in that class for part of the year."

"Violet, may I take you to lunch? I need to ask your forgiveness."

"For what?" She looked puzzled.

"I'll tell you at lunch, okay?"

We walked silently to the Union Building, through the cafeteria line, and to a table. "What do you need to talk to me about?"

"How much do you remember about our third grade class?" I asked.

"The music," she answered. "Our teacher played such beautiful music. I think she's the reason I'm a music minor today.

"It had been such a tough year for my family. My father died that July, and we found a little house to rent. It was so crowded with six children. I had to sleep with my two little sisters, and they both wet the bed. I can remember how embarrassed I was to come to school smelling so bad, but the bathtub didn't work, and we had to wash out of a washtub after heating the water on our coal stove. Usually there wasn't time to bathe in the morning." The words were tumbling out as Violet remembered bitterly that third grade experience. "I used to come to school and hide in the back corner."

I was finding it harder and harder to confess. As Violet spoke, the coals were heaped higher and higher upon my head. At last she was silent. "Violet, do you remember the Christmas party?"

Tears formed in her eyes. "Oh, yes."

"Violet, can you ever forgive me? I was the one who wrote that terrible poem that sent you sobbing from the room."

48

She looked puzzled. "What poem? I was crying because I hadn't had a quarter to buy a gift and yet someone had given a gift to me. I couldn't stand the guilt and the shame."

"Violet, there was a card attached to your gift. On it I wrote a terrible poem. Don't you remember?"

Violet tipped her head back and laughed. "I couldn't read in the third grade. I don't think I even looked at your poem." Then the knife twisted. "What did it say?"

"Violet, it doesn't matter. Just forgive me, please."

"Come on, what was the poem?"

I chose not to compound my guilt with a lie, so I quoted it to her.

"It seems appropriate to me," she laughed. "I forgive you."

We finished lunch, and I walked out of the Union Building with a lighter heart. However, every December 23, I still do penance for the cruelty of youth.

Home
and
Family

*T*he Long Embrace

Randal A. Wright

A few years ago I attended a high school basketball game between two powerhouse teams vying for the championship of an important tournament. Lincoln High had garnered five Texas State championships in the 1980s and was ranked as the number one team in the state on this occasion. The opponent was Beaumont West Brook, led by Lukie Jackson, son of former Olympic and NBA All-Star Luke Jackson. Both teams gave it everything they had. West Brook held the lead from the beginning of the game, thanks to the twenty-seven points accumulated by Lukie Jackson. Then, with just a few seconds left in regulation play, Lincoln tied the score, and the game went into overtime. The West Brook team was able to gain a one point advantage over their opponents. It appeared they would hold the lead to win the game—a great upset. However, with less than thirty seconds to go, a Lincoln player drove to the basket and was fouled by Lukie. He made both free throws, and Lincoln won the game by one point. Lukie was visibly upset. To have played so hard, scored so many points, but then commit a foul that cost his team the game against the defending state champions was devastating.

I wondered what his dad was thinking. Would he yell at his boy for making a mistake that cost them the game? Then I turned around to see a huge man coming down the aisle toward the dejected player. It was Lukie's father. Surely Lukie would get a tongue lashing that many sons would receive in similar situations when the father was embarrassed by his son's actions. But when they met, Luke Jackson threw his arms around his son and, in front of thousands of people, held him tightly, patted him on the back, and quietly talked to him. I watched this touching scene, wondering what I would have done had he been my son. When the long embrace ended, Lukie's countenance had changed. He looked like his team had just won the state championship. He was smiling and happy as he went over to congratulate the winning team.

"I Loved Your Father"

ELAINE CANNON

I think often of the powerful lesson I learned (and have shared now countless times) from a wine salesman with Italian roots who told me his story while we were airplane-seat companions. He was the youngest of five little children when their mother died. The father was a highly successful wine merchant in the United States. He promptly went back to Italy to find a proper mother for his brood. He fell in love with a schoolteacher, brought her back to the United States, settled her comfortably in the family home, and went on about his demanding business of production and travel. She had two children of her own, and the years passed. At an elaborate celebration for the twenty-fifth wedding anniversary, my traveling companion learned a powerful secret. He said, "I was sitting with our rebellious teenagers and wondering how we were going to survive these years. I looked over at that remarkable woman who had become mother to me when I was a toddler. I wondered how she did what she did. How did she make us all feel loved until we knew no difference between her own children and the rest of us from a different mother? She loved us and I loved her!

54

I got up and went over to her to tell her so. Then I asked her how she did it—how did she make us all feel so blessedly loved?"

"What did she say?" I quickly asked, my head reeling with remembrance of numerous households struggling with similar problems.

He continued, "She said to me, 'Oh, son, I loved your father and so I loved his children.' That's the secret!"

He was weeping now as he told me. My own heart leapt to understand that this was the secret of life: we love the Father and then we will love his children.

$\mathcal{T}$he Boy Is Worth More Than the Cow

WAYNE B. LYNN

It seemed as though he had just pulled the covers over himself when his father called, "Cal! Get up! Time to be up and about! Get your chores done. I'll be in from the field in about an hour and then we'll have breakfast."

Cal heard the door close as his father stepped out into the morning darkness. Fighting the desire to curl back under the warm covers, he rolled to the edge of the bed and dropped his feet onto the cold floor. His eyes strained against the darkness as he reached near the foot of his bed and picked up his soiled Levi's. The mud from yesterday's labor in the field still clung to them. They were cold against his shivering body as he stepped into them. His bare feet were feeling around the floor for his stockings while he buttoned his Levi's.

An overwhelming self-pity swept over him as he located his stockings. They were caked with the sweat and dirt of several days and holes were widening in them in several places. He guessed there were clean ones around somewhere, but he sure didn't know where they were and he hadn't taken time to look.

His feelings of self-pity persisted while he worked the soiled socks over his cold feet.

Nobody cares about me! he thought to himself.

"Mother has been gone for more than two weeks now. If she cared anything for me, she wouldn't go off and leave us just because some lady is having a new baby. All Dad cares about is the crops or the pigs or those darned milk cows! If he's so fond of cows, why doesn't he milk them himself instead of making me do it?" Thus his thoughts continued while he groped his way cautiously toward the front door. The sharp morning air quickly drew the drowsiness from him.

Cal gathered up the milk pails from the shed and started toward the barn. He kicked a bucket lying in his path and sent it banging and whirling across the barn yard. This gave vent to some of his emotions, but his mood was still sullen.

"All Dad has to do is start up that old tractor and sit there while I do all the work! I have to haul the grain, pitch the hay, slop the hogs, and milk these darned old cows. Those cows had better not try anything this morning!" He said to himself, "If Belinda so much as raises her foot she'll really get it!"

As he crossed the corral, his horse, Dan, nickered from the shed and came trotting out to meet him. Cal broke open a bale of hay and kicked part of it toward the hay manger.

"That will take care of you, you old nuisance."

By the time Cal had fed the pigs, filled the water troughs and milked most of the cows, the sun had risen and was shining brightly. It warmed his back as he started milking the last cow, Belinda. He always saved the long milkers till last hoping that one day his father would step over the rail and say, "Hold it, Cal. I'll finish up for you."

"Fat chance that that would ever happen. Dad doesn't care about me. All he cares about is these darned cows."

The pail gave off a sharp ring as he forced in the pure white slivers of milk. Soon the sound softened as the rich milk, foaming white and fragrant, began to fill the pail.

Cal was nearly finished when he heard a voice. It sounded like Old Man Jones was here again. He was probably pestering Dad to sell him Belinda. He could hear Mr. Jones's voice rising above that of his father. They were standing on the other side of the milk shed, and Old Man Jones was saying, "I don't know why you are so stubborn, Harry! Why don't you want to sell me that cow?"

His father was quick to reply, "Because a man doesn't go around selling his best cows when he's trying to build up his herd. That's why, Elmer!"

Old Man Jones had pitched his voice to a shrill squeak that drowned out all other sound.

"If she's such a good cow, Harry," he squeaked, "then why do you let the kid milk her?"

Cal stopped milking. The silence seemed eternal while he listened for the reply.

"Because," his father spoke in a firm, quiet voice, "the boy is worth more than the cow."

Maybe it was the morning sun shining down on Cal's back, or perhaps it was the thoughts of his mother coming home soon, but, somehow, he felt warm all over. He gave one final tug on Belinda, tossed the milk stool toward the fence, picked up the milk pail, and strode briskly toward the house.

He was whistling his favorite tune.

*O*n Goals

EVALYN D. BENNETT

*A*s a young woman approaches marriage and child rearing, she sets up some lofty goals, hoping to make her newly established cottage a little bit of heaven. As the years roll by, these specific goals have to be reevaluated and changed with the changing times and circumstances.

My goals twenty years ago included these:

1. Keep an immaculate home that would be an ideal setting for the Spirit of our Heavenly Father to dwell. To do this, organize my work into daily routines with weekly, monthly, quarterly, and yearly tasks.
2. Read the newspaper daily and at least one excellent book a month so I can become well informed about the world around me.
3. Prepare well-balanced, attractive gourmet meals, experimenting with at least one new recipe a week.
4. Bear many children, who will be well dressed, well pressed, and well behaved.
5. Keep an optimistic outlook on life. At the end of every week try to evaluate what created in me good feelings or frustrations.
6. Tell my husband once a day that I love him.

The first two years of our marriage, before children, were like a fantasy. I was so organized, inventive, and adorable. We ate such creations as cordon bleu and capon under glass. Our discussions were stimulating, and the house was hygienically spotless—not a thing was out of place.

Then came the first child. With the demands of burping, changing, loving, bathing, rocking, washing, and praying, some of my goals needed to be modified. I had to give up my immaculate home. My revised goals now read:

1. As I pass a table, blow hard on the top to rearrange the dust.
2. Put the vacuum in the middle of the living room first thing in the morning so that anyone calling will think that sometime soon I intend to get the debris from the floor.

Then came the second child. With the demands of burping, changing, loving, bathing, rocking, washing, and praying, some of my goals needed to be modified. I had to give up my book reading. My revised goals now read:

1. But not my newspapers. Ann Lander's advice column is as good as a Psychology 101 class providing me with deep insights into human relationships. If I can glance at Dr. Rex Morgan on the comic page once a week, I can keep up with the latest medical technology.
2. To keep well informed, I rush to the door when I hear the mailman to discuss some pertinent problems: "Has the garbage been picked up down the street yet?"

Then came the third child. With the demands of burping, changing, loving, bathing, rocking, washing, and praying, some of my goals needed to be modified. I had to give up my elaborate cooking fests. My revised goal now read:

1. Serve one hot dish a day. This means that if I serve hot soup for lunch, I can get away with peanut butter and jelly sandwiches for dinner. When I do find an extra hour and want to ease some guilt, I cook up a storm—meat loaf, mashed potatoes (from packaged flakes), Jell-O salad, and Popsicles. The children always ask, "Who is coming to dinner?" or "Is it Thanksgiving already?"

Then came the fourth child. With the demands of burping, changing, loving, bathing, rocking, washing, and praying, some of my goals needed to be modified. I had to give up well-dressed children. My revised goal now read:

1. Dressed. If the diaper is hanging around the knees by noon, my neighbors know that I pinned it properly earlier in the day. I haven't seen the bottom of my ironing baskets for three years, and I don't see any relief in sight.

Then came the fifth child. With the demands of burping, changing, loving, bathing, rocking, washing, and praying, some of my goals needed to be modified.

1. My goal no longer reads, "Keep an optimistic outlook on life. At the end of every week try to evaluate what created in me good feelings or frustrations." It now says, "Keep my voice down until noon. At the end of the week, count my children to reconfirm I have five. Check my mind to see if I have lost it. Check my varicose veins to see if my legs will carry me through another crazy week."

My last goal, "Tell my husband once a day that I love him," now simply says, "Try to speak to my husband once a day." With Cub Scouts, Little League, preschool, Virginia Tanner dance lessons, violin lessons, PTA board meetings, United Fund drive, Primary Blazers, Relief Society visiting teaching, University Women's Club, chicken pox, roseola, hepatitis, Asian flu, and tonsillectomies, I feel lucky to call out to him as we rush past each other going in and out of the front door, "Golly, dear, I am overdrawn at the bank again."

Twenty years later, my goals are really summarized in the phrase, "Sustain life and endure to the end." And a good pair of support hose certainly helps.

A Father Reading the Bible

Felicia Dorothea Browne Hemans

Twas early day, and sunlight streamed
  Soft through a quiet room,
That hushed, but not forsaken seemed,
  Still, but with naught of gloom.
For there, serene in happy age
  Whose hope is from above,
A father communed with the page
  Of heaven's recorded love.

Pure fell the beam, and meekly bright,
  On his gray holy hair,
And touched the page with tenderest light,
  As if its shrine were there!
But oh! that patriarch's aspect shone
  With something lovelier far—
A radiance all the spirit's own,
  Caught not from sun or star.

Some word of life e'en then had met
  His calm, benignant eye;
Some ancient promise, breathing yet
  Of immortality!
Some martyr's prayer, wherein the glow
  Of quenchless faith survives:
While every feature said—*"I know
  That my Redeemer lives!"*

And silent stood his children by,
   Hushing their very breath,
Before the solemn sanctity
   Of thoughts o'ersweeping death.
Silent—yet did not each young breast
   With love and reverence melt?
O! blest be those fair girls, and blest
   That home where god is felt!

Watching Katie

GEORGE D. DURRANT

I used to love basketball with a deep passion. I mean, I really liked it. It took precedence over ninety percent of the rest of my life's activities.

That is the way I felt when my second little grandchild, Katie, was two years old. Katie is a little redhead, but other than that she is a typical little child.

I was tending her on a Saturday afternoon while her parents were at the movies. I stayed home gladly with her because she was due for a nap and there was an NCAA tournament game on. Ralph Samson was the big star at the time. I loved to see him play, and this was a semifinal game. I was keyed up about watching it from the beginning to the end.

But, to my great distress, Katie would not go to sleep. She cried and begged to get up from her crib. I could deal with that because I could hold her on my lap while I watched the game. That worked until just before tip-off. But then I was greatly distressed because she went to the door and began an impassioned appeal to go outside. I tried everything that I could think of to dissuade her from wanting to go to a place where I could not see the TV. But it was no use; I had to go with her.

It was then that a miracle occurred. A genuine miracle. For as we walked down the front steps to the sidewalk, I realized that the game would still be played even if I wasn't there to watch it. That profound thought led to another one. And that was the amazing realization that I really didn't care as much as I had thought I would about not being able to see the game. Holding Katie's tiny hand and having her look up at me caused me to sense that what I was doing was much more important than seeing a ball swish through a net.

As we walked along it was a clear, wonderful, early spring day. At every house we passed, Katie would turn in and walk up the sidewalk to the porch. Arriving at the doorstep, she would turn back. I never gave her any direction, I just went wherever she wanted to go. Finally, after going a block away, she turned back toward home. Again we went up each sidewalk. Then we came to a little ditch. And I, to her great amusement, threw some rocks into the water. She laughed at each splash, and so did I. Finally we arrived back home. The game had just ended. To my surprise, I realized that the same team had won who would have won had I been there to watch. To this day I don't know who the winner was. But I can see in my mind every house that Katie led me to, and I can still see the rocks splashing into the water. I can still feel her tiny hand holding on to my extended finger. And when I see those things in my mind, it is like being in heaven.

Dad Will Come

ARDETH G. KAPP

I remember one evening years ago, while attending a Sunday School party, I looked at the clock, and it was past the time I was told to be home. Just then a knock came on the door. I was horrified—my dad had come after me. I felt humiliated in front of my friends. I thought I wanted to die. I was not pleasant with my dad; disobedience never makes one pleasant.

A few years later, my friends and I were driving home from a dance across an Indian reservation, ten miles from any shelter. It was 40 degrees below zero, and the windchill continued to lower the temperature. A few miles farther into the blizzard, we discovered that there was no heat in the car. Then the car froze up and would not run. We came to a slow stop. We watched the snow swirling in front of us only until the windows quickly froze over. We were quiet and sober as we contemplated our fate—our lives were in danger. The silence was broken as a friend in the backseat asked, "How long do you think it will be before your dad will get here?"

Why do you think they thought my dad would come? One time I had thought I wanted to die because he had come after me. This time we lived because my dad came through the blizzard to save my life and the lives of my friends. This time I was pleasant with my dad—pleasant and very grateful.

As Children See Us

Bryant S. Hinckley

Three hundred and twenty-six school children of a district near Indianapolis were asked to write anonymously just what each thought of his father.

The teacher hoped that the reading of the essays might attract the fathers to attend at least one meeting of the Parent-Teachers Association.

It did.

They came in $400 cars and $4,000 cars. Bank president, laborer, professional man, clerk, salesman, meter reader, farmer, utility magnate, merchant, baker, tailor, manufacturer, and contractor, every man with a definite estimate of himself in terms of money, skill, and righteousness or looks.

They sat spellbound as the president read a tribute to a stepfather, a tragic revelation of blight caused by white mule liquor and another woman, the description of the dream father of a widow's child, a dozen vague allusions to stranger-fathers, gone early, home late with time for nothing but food, reading and sleep, some timid pieces written in fear of a quick temper and a heavy hand.

But the sky cleared. The president picked at random from another stack of papers. "I like my daddy," she read from each. The reasons were many: he built my doll house, took me coasting, taught me to shoot, helps with my schoolwork, takes me to the park, gave me a pig to fatten and sell. Scores of essays could be reduced to: "I like my daddy. He plays with me."

Not one child mentioned his family house, car, neighborhood, food, or clothing.

The fathers went into the meeting from many walks of life; they came out in two classes: companions to their children or strangers to their children.

No man is too rich or too poor to play with his children.

"𝒥Am Waiting for You"

Marion D. Hanks

A daughter and I were recently discussing her return home at an hour that seemed questionable to me. I shared with her an experience with my wonderful mother. I had spent some years away at schools and missions and wars, and the two of us were now alone at home. I returned from an appointment one evening at midnight to find the light still on in Mother's little bedroom. As I had always done, I reported in to Mom, sat on her bed, and kidded with her a little. I asked her why she was still awake. "I am waiting for you," she said.

I said, "Did you wait for me while I was on a mission. Mom, or at sea, or in battle?"

Her answer was calm and sweet. She gave me that little pat on the knee that reflects the mature compassion of the wise for the ignorant, and said: "No, that would have been foolish. I just knelt down here by my bed and talked to the Lord about my boy. I told him what kind of man I believed you to be and wanted you to be, and prayed for his watchful care of you, and then left you in his hands and went to sleep. But now you are home," she said, "and you can count on it that I will be interested in you as long as I live."

The Perfect Dinner Table

Edgar A. Guest

A table cloth that's slightly soiled
Where greasy little hands have toiled;
The napkins kept in silver rings,
And only ordinary things
From which to eat, a simple fare,
And just the wife and kiddies there,
And while I serve, the clatter glad
Of little girl and little lad
Who have so very much to say
About the happenings of the day.

Four big round eyes that dance with glee,
Forever flashing joys at me,
Two little tongues that race and run
To tell of troubles and of fun;
The mother with a patient smile
Who knows that she must wait awhile
Before she'll get a chance to say
What she's discovered through the day.
She steps aside for girl and lad
Who have so much to tell their dad.

Our manners may not be the best;
Perhaps our elbows often rest
Upon the table, and at times
That very worst of dinner crimes,
That very shameful act and rude
Of speaking ere you've downed your food,
Too frequently, I fear, is done,

So fast the little voices run.
Yet why should table manners stay
Those tongues that have so much to say?

At many a table I have been
Where wealth and luxury were seen,
And I have dined in halls of pride,
Where all the guests were dignified;
But when it comes to pleasure rare
The perfect dinner table's where
No stranger's face is ever known:
The dinner hour we spend alone,
When little girl and little lad
Run riot telling things to dad.

ℐroposal

MURIEL JENKINS HEAL

To her his words of love
Were ripples on the sea,
Or rainbows hung from sunshine's rays
When rain clouds ceased their sovereignty.

She smiled a tear away
And turned to hide another,
But squeezed a reply to the tiny voice
That asked, "Will you marry me, Mother?"

$\mathcal{D}$o unto Others

RICHARD M. SIDDOWAY

★ 11-22-04

Would you do me a favor?" asked my friend Thomas. "I have this couple I've been trying to counsel, and they just won't listen to me. They both know you. I think you taught them both about fifteen years ago. Anyway, they said they'd like to talk with you. What do you think? Willing to give it a shot?"

Thomas and I had rekindled our long-time friendship a few years back, and every few weeks our families did something together. Then Thomas was called as the bishop of his ward. With the time demands of his calling, our get-togethers became fewer and farther apart. The following spring I was called as bishop in my ward. The meetings between our families became even less frequent.

And now came a phone call with the request that I help him counsel a couple in his ward. "For you, anything. Tell me who they are and what the problem is."

Thomas asked me if I remembered Wally Franklin. "Of course," I said. "Who could forget him? He was probably the brightest kid I ever taught."

"He thought you might remember him. He married Gayle Johnson about three or four years ago. They have a little girl about a year old. They're just kind of, well, tired of being married. I've tried talking to them, but they think I'm too old-fashioned or something. Anyway, they both mentioned your name, and I thought it was worth a shot. I'll tell them you're willing to see them. When's a good time?"

I checked my calendar and suggested some possible times. Thomas said he'd have the Franklins get back to me. Ten minutes later the phone rang again, and Gayle Franklin asked if she could visit with me the following Sunday evening.

Gayle Johnson, I thought. *Cheerleader, full of fun, never too dedicated to her studies but enough that she was eligible to stay on the cheerleading squad.* I hadn't thought about her in years, but my mind went back to basketball games in which she led the team onto the court with a yell followed by five or six back flips. She was the stereotypic cheerleader—frothy, fun, and full of energy. The high point of her high school experience seemed to revolve around decorating lockers and delivering cookies or cakes to team members before the "big game." She changed boyfriends as often as she changed shoes. Each one deserved her full attention for at least two weeks. Then she moved on to the next one.

One day stuck out in my memory—the day we dissected sharks in my science class. Gayle took one look at the dogfish shark lying in its dissecting pan, sniffed its preservative, and said, "Ooh, I can't touch that thing. It smells terrible." She squeezed her nose between thumb and forefinger and pretended to faint. After putting on rubber gloves she did the most careful dissection I had seen all year. Every cut was done with surgical precision and every organ carefully isolated and identified. When it was time to clean up, Gayle carefully wrapped her shark in wet cheesecloth. "How much more time do we get?" she asked.

"Tomorrow," I replied.

"Can I come in after school and work on it? I don't think I can finish tomorrow." She worked nearly two hours after school. Many of her classmates had butchered their way to completion in the one class period. I began to wonder how much of Gayle's personality was an act.

Wally Franklin had been both a joy and a frustration. Wally absorbed information faster than a sponge absorbs water. He had a great memory and quick recall. Whenever we started a new concept in class, Wally reached the conclusion five minutes later. The rest of the class took considerably longer. Wally frequently became impatient with the rest of the class and wanted to move on. I began giving Wally individual research projects to do. He'd check in at the first of class, discover what we were doing that day, then slip out and go to the library.

There was only one question Wally ever missed on a test, and that created some controversy. While the class was studying the Krebs citric-acid cycle from our year-old textbook, Wally was studying it from an older book in the library. A slight correction in the cycle had been made between the two versions, and Wally missed the question on the test. He insisted that he be given credit, since he could document his answer. The fact that the "facts" had changed seemed irrelevant to Wally.

What in the world drew these two people together? I wondered. Frothy, little Gayle and tall, gangly Wally must have somehow drifted together. *Well,* I thought, *opposites attract.*

Sunday evening our Scoutmaster and one of my counselors were checking in money from the Scout sustaining membership drive, when Gayle Franklin appeared at my office door. They excused themselves and moved into the clerk's office.

"Would you give me just a moment, Gayle?" I asked. I closed the door and knelt beside my desk. *Help me, please, to be of help to this young couple.* I prayed a few more minutes, then rose and opened the door. Gayle extended her hand and shook mine.

"Thanks for seeing me, Mr. Sid—I guess that should be Bishop, shouldn't it?" She giggled nervously.

"Call me anything that feels comfortable, Gayle. It's been nearly ten years, hasn't it?"

"Actually, it's been about twelve, I think. Let's see . . ." And she began counting on her fingers the years since she graduated. "Oh, but I was a junior when I had your class, so that means . . ." She went on figuring. Gayle had been a pretty little cheerleader; she had blossomed into a beautiful young woman. As she sat in the chair across from me on the other side of the desk, it seemed that everything about her was as perfect as she could make it. Not a hair was out of place. There were no wrinkles on her face or in her clothing. She chattered on for a few minutes.

"Gayle, why don't you fill me in on what has happened in your life since I last saw you? I suppose quite a bit has happened in the last ten or eleven or twelve years, hasn't it?"

She inhaled a lungful of air and let out a mighty sigh. "After graduation I went off to school. I decided I wanted to be a doctor, but my grades weren't good enough and I couldn't get accepted into the pre-med program. They suggested I might transfer to another school that didn't have such tough requirements. Instead, I changed my major and went into sociology. I figured if I couldn't heal bodies, maybe I could help heal society. After a while I discovered I really didn't like sociology, and I changed majors again. I probably changed my major a half dozen times in the next three years. While I was going to school I started working at a furniture store as a salesclerk. I discovered I had a flair for design. Pretty soon I was helping people decorate their houses. I dropped out of college and began my own little decorating company."

She paused and looked me straight in the face. "Pretty silly, huh?"

"Not at all. Are you still running your business?" I asked.

"Not really. Oh, I still do some decorating as a favor to a friend. But since we got married, Wally wants me to stay home. I don't do much of it anymore." She paused and seemed to take intense interest in the file cabinet in the corner of my office.

I took advantage of the pause. "How did you and Wally meet? Tell me about that."

"That was kind of funny. Wally's mother asked me to help her decorate for a wedding—Wally's older sister, maybe you remember Donna Jo?" I nodded that I rememberd her. "I was there at their house, wearing some terrible outfit—Levi's and a sweatshirt, I think—when Wally walked in. I hadn't seen him since high school. He helped me with the decorations, and then about a week after the wedding he called me and asked me to go out to dinner. We dated for about a year and then got married." Her eyes were filling with tears. I offered her a box of Kleenex.

"Go on," I said.

Gayle dabbed at the tears with a tissue. "At first we were happy enough, and miserable, if you know what I mean. I guess it doesn't matter how long you date someone, you really don't know him until you get married." I nodded my head in agreement. "Do you know what our first fight was about? Whether you have to put a salad fork on the table if you're not having salad." She smiled through her tears. "Pretty stupid, huh?"

"Lots of people argue about where you squeeze the toothpaste tube," I offered. "In retrospect these things seem pretty stupid, but at the time they appear to be major problems."

"I don't want to sound like we fought all the time. We really didn't. I think basically we were pretty happy. When I discovered I was pregnant, we were both overjoyed."

"Was it an easy pregnancy?" I asked.

"I had morning sickness twenty-four hours a day for nearly four months," she laughed. "Wally really pitched in and helped. When Alicia was born it seemed like our marriage was finally complete. But in the last year Wally has changed so much." Suddenly her face clouded and the tears began falling again. "I'm sorry," she choked through the sobs.

"Just take your time," I said. "Tell me about Wally, how he's changed."

A few minutes passed. "Well, when we were dating—I mean, here I was this dumb little girl, and he was the smartest kid I'd ever known. And he was really considerate. I mean, he'd open the door for me, and ask me what I wanted to do. And now . . . oh, I don't know. Now he's so demanding. I think he resents Alicia. He's always after me to leave her with a baby-sitter and she's only fourteen months old."

"How often do you leave her?" I asked.

"Never. She's not old enough yet. I wouldn't be here tonight if Wally weren't home with her."

"I see. What else has Wally done that makes you so unhappy?"

"He just never has time for me anymore. I don't know, I just don't think he wants to be married to me." She used up half a dozen more tissues. "He's just changed. I want more out of our marriage than I'm getting." She pushed herself from the chair. "I'm sorry. I've taken too much of your time. Thanks for listening."

I arose from my chair and walked around the desk. "Let me ask you two questions. Would you like to come and talk with me again? And do you think Wally would like to come?"

"Why? Do you think there's any way to save our marriage?" I heard the sound of defeat in her voice.

"Perhaps. Would you like to come again?" She nodded her head. "And Wally, do you think he'd come?" She shrugged her shoulders. "Please ask him," I said as I let her out the door.

I sank to my knees and offered another prayer for guidance. A feeling of peace came over me.

I was still working in my office an hour later, when the phone rang. "Bishop, this is Wally Franklin. If you have time, I'd like to talk to you." I assured him I'd take the time. Ten minutes later there was a knock on my door. It opened and in walked Wally.

"It's been a long time," I said, extending my hand. Wally shook it.

"Thanks for making time for me. I know you're not really our bishop and you really don't have to get involved, but I appreciate your taking time."

"My pleasure. How are you doing?"

"Pretty well, I guess. My engineering firm seems to have really taken off. We have more work than we can handle."

"I didn't know you were an engineer, but it doesn't surprise me. You were always such a good student."

"Thanks, Bishop. I really have fond memories of you. I don't think anybody else would have let me study on my own. And I'll never forget what you told me on graduation night."

I couldn't remember even seeing Wally at his graduation. In fact, after more than twenty years of commencements, I had trouble keeping them separate. "What was that, Wally?"

"You said, 'Wally, you can be anything you want to be.' I could tell you meant it. You know, I went off to college and met a lot of other really bright kids. There were times when I wanted to give it all up, and I'd remember what you said."

I didn't want to tell Wally that I'd said the same thing to thousands of students. Of course, it is pretty good advice.

"I went on a mission. Served in Brazil. Portuguese came pretty easy to me, but I really struggled with some of my companions. Some of them really didn't want to work. Maybe I was just being too hard on them. Anyway, I came home and finished school. I was hired by a good engineering firm. I stayed with them for about two years, then struck out on my own. We've done really well."

"Do you remember Gayle Johnson?" he asked. I nodded. "She came to my house to help decorate for my sister's wedding. Did you ever teach Donna Jo?"

"I remember her, Wally, but I didn't have her in class."

"Well, Gayle came to our house to decorate for Donna Jo's wedding. I've never felt really sure of myself around girls, especially really pretty ones like Gayle, but she asked me to help her with some of the decorations. After the wedding she told me she'd like to get together sometime. One thing led to another, and about a year later we got married in the Salt Lake Temple.

"We had all of her family and all of my family there. It was quite a gathering." Wally's somber face broke into just a hint of smile. "We've had a pretty good marriage," he conceded, "until this last year. Boy, has Gayle changed!"

"In what way, Wally?"

He examined the file cabinet with his eyes. "When Gayle was first pregnant—oh, I forgot to tell you, we have a little girl, Alicia—when Gayle was pregnant with her she was really sick and she let me help her. Gayle really likes to do things her way. You could tell if you visited our house. She usually won't let me help her with much of anything, but she was sick enough that she let me get in and help. But since Alicia was born, wow, I just have to get out of the way. I think Gayle would be happier if I weren't there. I thought temple marriages were supposed to be happy."

"Wally, we do a great job of preparing people to get married in the temple. We do a lousy job of preparing people to get married. Sometimes we focus so much on the temple, that we don't tell people what it's like to be married. Two people come to a marriage from different backgrounds. Each is convinced the whole world lives and behaves the way his or her family does. Then they get married and find they do things differently. Does that make sense?"

"Bishop, I know just what you mean. Do you know what our first argument was about?" I thought I did—something to do with a salad fork—but I shook my head. "Which side of the dresser was hers and which was mine. I grew up sharing a room with my brother, and I always had the left side of the dresser. Well, it turns out Gayle always had the left side of the dresser, too."

"How did you resolve it?" I asked.

"I gave in. I always have to give in. Gayle always wants things done her way. Period."

"You feel you always have to do things her way," I said.

"Yes! Well, most of the time. And she sends contradictory messages. I mean, she's always complaining about being stuck in the house with the baby, but she won't go anywhere without Alicia."

"You feel like you don't know what she really wants," I said.

"Bishop, I just feel like I ought to be getting more out of our marriage than I'm getting. Am I wrong?" He rose to go.

"Wally, let me ask you two questions. First, would you like to come and talk to me again, and second, do you think Gayle would come and talk to me?"

"I feel like I've taken too much of your time as it is," he said.

"Wally, would you like to come again?"

He thought for a moment. "If you think it would really do any good."

"What about Gayle? Do you think she'd come?"

He shrugged his shoulders. "I can ask."

After Wally left I called my friend Thomas. "I've just talked to the Franklins. What do you think their basic problem is?"

"Well, I don't think either one wants to change. They both want the other one to do all the changing. What do you think?"

"I think you've summed it up pretty well," I said. "I've asked them to come and see me again. I'll keep you posted."

For the third time that night I sank to my knees and asked for help. Although a feeling of peace came, I felt no clear direction as to what I could do.

Two days later Gayle called. "When would you have time to see me?"

"We'll be in the church for Mutual tonight," I said. "How about eight-thirty?"

"Fine. Wally will be home by then to take care of Alicia. See you then."

The joint activity involving the young men and women in my ward was ending. The kids were standing around the cultural hall eating Astro bars, a favorite frozen confection from a local drive-in, when I spotted Gayle in the foyer outside my office. I excused myself from the activity and went to greet her. "Just a minute, Gayle."

I entered my office and sank to my knees. *Father, I need help. These are two fine young people. Please, please help me know what I should say to help them.*

A powerful feeling of peace came over me. The Spirit whispered, *Love them.*

I invited Gayle into my office. After we seated ourselves, she said, "I understand Wally came to talk to you."

"That's right." Suddenly the words began to tumble from my mouth. "I've given quite a bit of thought to your situation since the other night. I could try to be gentle about this, but I'm going to be straightforward. I don't think your marriage has a chance in the world of succeeding." I sat upright in my chair. What in the world was I saying?

Her mouth dropped open. I saw tears well up in her eyes. "No chance? None at all?" she said.

"Gayle, I want to be your friend and I'm going to give you some advice. I think six months from now your marriage will be over. I've talked to Wally and I don't think he's willing to change at all. I want you to look ahead to what's going to happen at the time of the divorce. Wally is going to try to take Alicia away from you, and I think you need to protect yourself."

"No chance at all?" she said again.

"Gayle, listen to me. There's only one way you can protect yourself and your daughter. When Wally goes to court, he's going to paint you as the most uncooperative woman in the world. He's going to say that you are selfish and that you were totally unwilling to meet his needs or his desires. Do you understand what I'm saying?"

She nodded her head. "What do I do?"

"Gayle, what I'm going to ask you to do will be the hardest thing you've ever done in your life. I want you to promise me that whatever Wally asks you to do for the next six months, you'll do. Everything! Do you understand me?"

"Yes, but why?

"Because when you go into court and you battle for the rights to this precious little girl of yours, your attorney is going to be able to say about you, 'She did everything this man asked her to do, and it's still not enough.' Do you love your little girl enough to do what I'm suggesting?"

"Oh yes. Are you sure I won't lose her?"

"Gayle, there are no guarantees, but I can tell you you'll have a much better chance of keeping her. There's one other part to this deal. You cannot, absolutely cannot, tell Wally what you're doing, or he'll be able to use it against you. Do you understand?"

Her eyes fell to the carpet. "I don't know if I can do it. It's going to be so hard."

"It's only for six months. You can do anything for six months, can't you?"

"I can," she said with resolve. "I'll do everything Wally asks me to do and I won't tell him a thing. I'm not going to let him get Alicia."

"Gayle, I'm serious about this. I want you to promise me you'll do what I said. I'll always be here for you if you need to talk."

"I promise. I promise! Oh, I wish there were some other way."

I helped her to her feet and sent her out the door. The feeling of peace grew even stronger. Quickly I called their home. "Wally, can you come and see me as soon as Gayle gets home.

I think we have to have a pretty serious conversation." He agreed to come. A few minutes later his car pulled into the parking lot, and soon there was a knock on my door. "Come in, Wally."

He burst into my office. "What's the matter, Bishop?"

"Have a seat, Wally." He seated himself slowly. "I have just finished talking with Gayle. I wish I had better news, but I'm convinced your marriage is over. Within six months you'll find yourself in divorce court and Gayle will be trying to take Alicia from you."

He leapt from his seat. "Not without a fight!"

"Wally, she's going to win because she's going to go into court and paint you as a man who is demanding and unwilling to change. She's going to tell the judge that you were totally unresponsive to her needs. I've been your friend for a long time, and I think you need to protect yourself. Here's what I'm asking you to do. For the next six months, whenever Gayle asks you to do anything, you do it. Treat her like a queen. Then when your court date arrives you can show that you have done everything in your power to keep your wife happy. Do you understand?"

As I spoke, he sank slowly into his chair. "You're right," he said. "She's going to make it look like I'm the one to blame. Bishop, you've got a deal. From this moment I pledge to do everything and anything my wife wants. What else?"

"Wally, you can't tell her what you are doing. You can never let it slip that you are doing this to prove you are a worthy husband and father, or she'll bring it up in court and it will explode in your face! Do you understand?"

He stood up quickly. "I understand perfectly. She's going to get a perfect husband and never know what it's all about. Thanks for looking out for me, Bishop." He walked quickly to the door.

"Wally, I'm always here if you need to talk."

He climbed into his car and drove away. I sank to my knees. *Well done,* whispered the Spirit.

I called my friend Thomas. "I tried to work out a solution. I think you'll need to keep a pretty careful eye on the Franklins." He agreed.

I heard nothing more from him or the Franklins for nearly four months, when I bumped into Gayle at the grocery store. "How are you two getting along?"

"Bishop, you were wrong. I took your advice, but Wally and I aren't getting a divorce. I can't imagine why you thought our marriage was at end. He's the most considerate husband and father I've ever seen. He treats me like a queen."

I'm sure Wally feels he is married to one. The Lord works in mysterious ways, his wonders to perform.

"Grandpa, Are You Awake?"

GEORGE D. DURRANT

Grandpa. Grandpa! *Grandpa!* Are you awake?"

If I hadn't been, I was now. It was five-thirty in the morning in Houston, Texas. Just two days after Christmas.

As I forced open my eyes, I saw my four-year-old grandson, Kolby, standing at my side and studiously staring at me to see if there were any signs of life. Seeing his face through the dimness of the early morning light was like seeing the sun come up, and suddenly I could answer with great enthusiasm, "Yes, sirree, Kolby! Your grandpa is wide awake."

"Get up, Grandpa. It's time to play."

Five minutes later I was sitting on the front room floor pushing Thomas the Tank Engine down his wooden track as Kolby, who sat at my side, drew Thomas on his Etch A Sketch. It was for moments like this that I had made the long journey from my home in Provo, Utah, to Kolby's house in Houston,

Texas. It was for moments like this that I thanked the Lord for the joy and privilege of being Grandpa.

As I looked at what my grandson was drawing on the Etch A Sketch, I was intrigued by how that little machine worked, and I said to Kolby, "I get to play with the Etch A Sketch next. Okay?"

"Okay, Grandpa. I'll be through in a minute. Then I'll let you have a turn. Right now you just keep pushing Thomas, okay?"

"Okay," I said with a little feeling of impatience.

As I looked at Kolby's excited expression my heart welled up with love for him, and I reached out and pulled him close to me and said, "Grandpa needs a hug from his friend named Kolby."

"Don't hug me right now, Grandpa. You made me make a line that I didn't want to make."

As he pulled away I asked him, "How come I love you so much, Kolby?"

He laughed and said, "I don't know." He then quickly added, "Maybe it is because I let you play with my toys." I smiled and thought to myself, *That is only a part of the reason. There is more to it than that. Much more.* But this serious thought was not for now, so I turned and pushed Thomas the Tank Engine down the track past Sir Topham Hatt, the railroad superintendent.

I found myself being glad that Kolby's parents were still sound asleep. We had all been up late the night before, and so they needed their rest. But the greatest reason I was glad was that I could have Kolby all to myself. And that was a bit like being in heaven without dying. The only thing that marred those golden moments was my longing to get hold of the Etch a Sketch. And maybe soon even that would happen.

Faith
and
Trust

The Boy and the Mango Tree

John H. Groberg

Editor's Note: Elder John H. Groberg was a young elder in the Tonga mission during the 1950s, where he learned many lessons in faith with his loyal native companion, Feki.

Shortly after moving into our house, I received a great lesson in Tongan faith. It happened like this: the day was hot, the mangoes were ripe, and life moved slowly forward. Feki and I had just returned from visiting when suddenly we heard some yelling and knew something unusual had happened.

The noise of a small crowd was getting closer to our house. We went outside to see what was going on just as a member, his family, and a few others arrived at our *fale*.

The father carried the seemingly lifeless body of his little ten-year-old boy wrapped in a large *tupenu* (piece of cloth). As the father lowered him from his shoulder and put him into my arms, he said, "He has fallen from high in a mango tree and hit his head and back on the hard roots. Here, make him well and bring him back to me."

I looked at the limp body and said, "He's dead. What can I do?" The father just looked at me and said, "Whether he's dead or not, I do not know. What I do know is I want him well again, and you have the power to do it."

I said, "Life is from God. If God has allowed his life to leave, we should be reconciled." He responded, "I've talked to God. I want my boy back now more than God wants him now. Make him well. It's fine."

I didn't know the words in Tongan to administer to his son, and I was looking for some way to get out of this uncomfortable situation. I had not personally experienced this type of faithful determination before and I just wanted to leave, but the look of expectation on the faces of his father, mother, brothers, sisters, and friends was so intense that I felt tremendous pressure to do something.

"We should get the branch president," I said, stalling for time. No sooner had I said this than the branch president walked up. He had been working in his garden when he heard the disturbance and came to see what was happening.

Feki quickly explained the situation. In a sort of panic-stricken state, I said, "You're the branch president. This is your responsibility."

I tried to give the child to him, but he said, "No, just hold him. I'm going to shower, clean up, and put on my Sunday clothes. Then we'll administer to him, and we'll see what God's will is."

I couldn't believe him. I complained, "He's dead, or dying, and you want to clean up first?" He looked at me with compassion (and maybe a little disdain for my lack of faith) and replied, "It is a sacred work to administer to someone. I am not going to approach God all sweaty and in my dirty clothes."

I waited for what seemed hours (but was probably less than ten minutes). Everyone else was calm and quiet, but my heart was pounding fiercely. There was no movement from the child. Finally the branch president emerged in his clean white clothes with a bottle of olive oil. Feki, who was a priest, helped me with the Tongan words as I anointed the boy, and the branch president sealed the anointing and blessed him.

I didn't understand all of the words of the blessing, but I did understand when the branch president finished and said to me, "Take the boy. Pray. Exercise your faith, and it will be according to God's will, his parent's faith, and your faith."

In all this time, I had not felt a heartbeat or breathing or any movement from the boy. I despaired as all eyes turned to me.

The logic of my thinking was to tell them, "Dig a grave. This boy is dead. Don't make me do this."

But the faith of the Tongans caused me to go into our house with Feki, carrying the boy's limp body. It was almost evening. We closed the door, let the blinds down, and sat there in a sort of stupor as I thought of the father's last words, "We'll wait right here for as long as it takes. Just bring my boy back to me alive and well." I laid the boy wrapped in his *tupenu* on the floor. I could see no movement at all.

I have been scared on many occasions—such as car crashes, near drownings, scholastic tests, and the like—but I'm not sure I have ever been more scared than at that moment. This was life. This was faith. This was priesthood power on the line. And there was only me, my companion, a seemingly life-less body—and God.

I prayed as I had never prayed before, "Help me out of this. What should I do?" Tears followed—tears of sorrow for the family and the boy and also tears of fear. What could I do? My faith simply was not strong enough. Feki sat in the corner wait-ing silently.

Little by little the fog of my mental despair began to dissi-pate. I began to feel: This is God's work. I am on His mission. The branch president holds the priesthood. So do I. These people have faith. God wouldn't leave us without some way out. These people can be made to understand. It won't be that bad. Something will work out somehow.

Then I reflected: God lives and loves us. Jesus lives and loves us. He healed the sick. He brought back the dead. As my mind caught hold of that thought, a light began to appear. Fear began to recede. Faith began to motivate my prayers.

The more earnestly I prayed, the brighter the light became. My thought was no longer, "How do I get out of this?" but rather, "What is God's will? What should I do? I'll do it, no mat-ter what it is." I felt much better. I was still shaking, but light and courage were now replacing darkness and fear.

Time went by, then a very faint impression came, "Give him

artificial respiration." I waited, but the impression stayed. The only artificial respiration I remembered was when I was a Boy Scout and we learned to push on the back of the rib cage and say, "Out goes the bad air, in comes the good." It seemed silly, but I felt I should try. I didn't even think about the possible damage if he had broken bones. I turned him on his stomach and put his head to the side with his arms at right angles. I could sense the limp, cold feel of death, but I also felt the warmth and power of faith that seemed to be pouring through the very walls of our house.

I couldn't remember exactly what to do, except to push on his back and say, "Out goes the bad air," then release and say, "in comes the good," so that is what I did. For several minutes my hopes rose, but as time ticked by and nothing happened, that former dark feeling of fear began to return. "No!" I said. "Get away! You can't be here, not with their faith!"

Suddenly, I felt a little twitch. Was it one of my muscles? Silence. More artificial respiration. Another twitch. *That's not me,* I thought. Then another twitch, and another, more definite now. It must have been an hour since he was first placed in my arms with no sign of life. More artificial respiration. A stronger twitch, then all of a sudden a violent retching and a great gush of half-digested mango pieces and gastric juices spewed onto the floor. It came and came. There seemed to be more than it was possible for one little boy to hold.

The smell was terrible, yet sweet, for what did I notice as the retching subsided? Tiny shades of breathing? Slight rising and falling of the back? Could it be?

Faithful Feki moved from the corner and with a rag, a bucket, and water began cleaning up the mess.

The night wore on. At times I thought there was regular breathing. At other times I thought I was deceiving myself. Prayers ascended all night. The fight between the light of faith and the darkness of fear continued. Finally the first glimmerings of dawn began to appear. There was still no sustained movement. But as the daylight became a reality and the darkness faded away, so did the light of faith reign and the darkness of fear depart.

There was definitely a hint of breathing and a little warmth where his heart was. We had no thought of eating or drinking, just fasting and praying and the spiritual sustenance of faith to keep us going. Throughout the day we could hear the family outside, but never once did they complain or even inquire. They just waited, prayed, and believed.

Again, twilight came. But as the light receded and the soft cover of darkness enveloped our small *fale,* this time it did not bring with it fear but rather a sweet assurance that things would be all right.

The prayers continued, increasing in faith through the second night. We kept up a constant *mili mili* (rubbing or massaging of the back). Finally, as the light returned the second morning, there was a little movement of the boy's head, a tentative moan, and a tiny flutter of the eyelids. As the first sunbeams of the light came through the cracks of the coconut frond blinds and streamed across the floor up to the young boy's face, almost on cue his eyes popped open. He looked about for a moment, still without moving, and simply said, " *'Oku ou 'ife?"* (Where am I?")

His eyes closed again for a while, then reopened. His head moved. He rolled over on his back, then on his side. He tried to get up but couldn't. He was too weak to walk, but he was alive! I picked him up and carried him to his parents outside. As Feki opened the door, the whole family stood waiting. I simply handed the little boy back to his father and said, *"He'e, ko ho foha. Kuo sai."* ("Here is your son. He is all right.")

With tears of gratitude, they thanked me profusely. With as much sincerity as I have ever felt, I replied, "Thank God, not me. He healed him. In an eternal sense, only He can truly heal. That is who the Savior is—the great Healer of all mankind and of all our problems. If we will only have faith in Him and do as He says, He will heal us all of all our problems." They listened respectfully.

It is hard to comprehend the feelings of that moment, for they were deep and full of love, faith, tears of joy, and the Spirit of God. Feki and I returned to our house, and after prayer we slept and slept and slept. No one bothered us. How sweet sleep is when you have done your duty and followed God's will—no matter what was required!

The Gardener and the Currant Bush

HUGH B. BROWN

In the early dawn, a young gardener was pruning his trees and shrubs. He had one choice currant bush which had gone too much to wood. He feared therefore that it would produce little, if any, fruit.

Accordingly, he trimmed and pruned the bush and cut it back. In fact, when he had finished, there was little left but stumps and roots.

Tenderly he considered what was left. It looked so sad and deeply hurt. On every stump there seemed to be a tear where the pruning knife had cut away the growth of early spring. The poor bush seemed to speak to him, and he thought he heard it say:

"Oh, how could you be so cruel to me; you who claim to be my friend, who planted me and cared for me when I was young, and nurtured and encouraged me to grow? Could you not see that I was rapidly responding to your care? I was nearly half as large as the trees across the fence, and might soon have become like one of them. But now you've cut my branches back; the green, attractive leaves are gone, and I am in disgrace among my fellows."

The young gardener looked at the weeping bush and heard its plea with sympathetic understanding. His voice was full of kindness as he said, "Do not cry; what I have done to you was necessary that you might be a prize currant bush in my garden. You were not intended to give shade or shelter by your branches. My purpose when I planted you was that you should bear fruit. When I want currants, a tree, regardless of its size, cannot supply the need.

"No, my little currant bush, if I had allowed you to continue to grow as you had started, all your strength would have gone to wood; your roots would not have gained a firm hold, and the purpose for which I brought you into my garden would have been defeated. Your place would have been taken by another, for you would have been barren. You must not weep; all this will be for your good; and some day, when you see more clearly, when you are richly laden with luscious fruit, you will thank me and say, 'Surely, he was a wise and loving gardener. He knew the purpose of my being, and I thank him now for what I then thought was cruelty.' "

Some years later, this young gardener was in a foreign land, and he himself was growing. He was proud of his position and ambitious for the future.

One day an unexpected vacancy entitled him to promotion. The goal to which he had aspired was now almost within his grasp, and he was proud of the rapid growth which he was making.

But for some reason unknown to him, another was appointed in his stead, and he was asked to take another post relatively unimportant and which, under the circumstances, caused his friends to feel that he had failed.

The young man staggered to his tent and knelt beside his cot and wept. He knew now that he could never hope to have what he had thought so desirable. He cried to God and said, "Oh, how could you be so cruel to me? You who claim to be my friend—you who brought me here and nurtured and encouraged me to grow. Could you not see that I was almost equal to the other men whom I have so long admired? But now I have been cut down. I am in disgrace among my fellows. Oh, how could you do this to me?"

He was humiliated and chagrined and a drop of bitterness was in his heart, when he seemed to hear an echo from the past. Where had he heard those words before? They seemed familiar. Memory whispered:

"I'm the gardener here."

He caught his breath. Ah, that was it—the currant bush! But why should that long-forgotten incident come to him in the midst of his hour of tragedy? And memory answered with words which he himself had spoken:

> "Do not cry . . . what I have done to you was necessary . . . you were not intended for what you sought to be, . . . if I had allowed you to continue . . . you would have failed in the purpose for which I planted you and my plans for you would have been defeated. You must not weep; some day when you are richly laden with experience you will say, 'He was a wise gardener. He knew the purpose of my earth life. . . . I thank him now for what I thought was cruel.'"

His own words were the medium by which his prayer was answered. There was no bitterness in his heart as he humbly spoke again to God and said, "I know you now. You are the gardener, and I the currant bush. Help me, dear God, to endure the pruning, and to grow as you would have me grow; to take my allotted place in life and ever more to say, "Thy will not mine be done."

Another lapse of time in our story. Forty years have passed. The former gardener and officer sits by his fireside with wife and children and grandchildren. He tells them the story of the currant bush—his own story; and as he kneels in prayer with them, he reverently says to God, "Help us all to understand the purpose of our being, and be ever willing to submit to thy will and not insist upon our own. We remember that in another garden called Gethsemane the choicest of all thy sons was glorified by submission unto thy will."

As they arose from prayer, this family group, they joined in singing a familiar hymn which now had for them new meaning.

"It may not be on the mountain height,
Or over the stormy sea,
It may not be at the battle's front,
My Lord will have need of me. . . .

So trusting my all to thy tender care,
And knowing thou lovest me,
I'll do thy will with a heart sincere,
I'll be what you want me to be."

The father closed "Home Evening" with the lines:

"My will not thine be done," turned paradise into
a desert.
"Thy will not mine," turned the desert into a
paradise, and made Gethsemane the gate of
heaven.

Drinking That Water Will Mean Death!

CHARLES R. WOODBURY

Many of the young men from our small town of Hinckley, Utah, were called to serve their country during the World War II conflict. Brother Terry, one of those young men from our ward, came home on furlough and had the privilege of going through the temple with his parents. When his furlough was over he was to be sent overseas into combat and he was quite concerned about it.

I had given him a patriarchal blessing some time before, so he came to me requesting a special blessing before going onto the battlefield. He came after much fasting and prayer, so I gave him the desired blessing in which I promised him, "Though you may not be privileged to wear the garments that were placed on you in the temple, as long as you keep those covenants sacred, you'll enjoy the same protection and blessing. You shall see your companions shot down by your side, but you shall not be injured. Your life will be preserved so that you might perform a great missionary work there. And," I said, "should the only water available to you become contaminated and pronounced by medical science as unfit to drink, if you will not partake of the things that are forbidden of the Lord, he will make the water sweeter to your taste than any water you ever drank and you shall be able to drink of it and it shall not injure you. Those about you will not understand the ways of the Lord and will marvel when they see you drink of that water and live. Remember, however, this blessing will come to you only by observing the Word of Wisdom and not partaking of those things the Lord has declared as not good for man."

It was a highly unusual blessing, but one that gave that young man peace and confidence that he would return unharmed to his loved ones. He then left to join his comrades in battle, knowing the Lord would be his protector.

When he returned from the war, he came and bore his testimony to me. "Twice our division went into action," he said. "The first time, there were five of our group who came back, myself and four others. The next time, three of us returned; the rest were slain.

"One time," he continued, "our water supply became contaminated and our medical men told us not to drink the water, for it would mean certain death. My buddies, of course, decided not to drink the polluted water, knowing that if they were to enjoy the momentary pleasure of quenching their thirst, they would not live long enough to enjoy the many pleasures that awaited those who would return home from the battlefields. But I trusted in the Lord and the blessing you gave me, which I knew was given through the spirit of revelation. I drank the water and have never tasted better water in my life—it was deliciously sweet and, more importantly, quenched my burning thirst. My companions were completely dismayed and distressed by my actions and feared that they would certainly witness my agonizing death within a very short time. Contrary to the statement of the medical authorities and to the wonderment of those about me, my health was not injured in any way and I was permitted to continue the work that I was asked to do in the service of my country and fellowmen.

"I then had a chance to explain the gospel to many of those boys who watched me drink that contaminated water without harmful effects and had wondered and marveled at how that could be. I gratefully took advantage of the opportunity to explain the Word of Wisdom to my much-perplexed companions and the power of the priesthood to give blessings of protection to those obedient to the principles of the gospel.

"This experience caused many of them to want to know more about the gospel of Jesus Christ and they began investigating the Church. I don't know how many of them finally accepted the gospel, as I soon finished my tour of duty and was sent home, but I do know that many of them were studying the scriptures and reading the literature I had given them that explained the Church of Jesus Christ and its principles."

His House

C. S. Lewis

I find I must borrow yet another parable from George MacDonald. Imagine yourself as a living house. God comes in to rebuild that house. At first, perhaps, you can understand what He is doing. He is getting the drains right and stopping the leaks in the roof and so on: you knew that those jobs needed doing and so you are not surprised. But presently he starts knocking the house about in a way that hurts abominably and does not seem to make sense. What on earth is He up to? The explanation is that He is building quite a different house from the one you thought of—throwing out a new wing here, putting on an extra floor there, running up towers, making courtyards. You thought you were going to be made into a decent little cottage: but He is building a palace. He intends to come and live in it Himself.

"Walk to the Edge of the Light"

Boyd K. Packer

I had been called as an Assistant to the Council of the Twelve, and we were to move to Salt Lake City and find an adequate and permanent home. President Henry D. Moyle assigned someone to help us.

A home was located that was ideally suited to our needs. Elder Harold B. Lee came and looked it over very carefully and then counseled, "By all means, you are to proceed."

But there was no way we could proceed. I had just completed the course work on a doctor's degree and was writing the dissertation. With the support of my wife and our eight children, all of the resources we could gather over the years had been spent on education.

By borrowing on our insurance, gathering every resource, we could barely get into the house, without sufficient left to even make the first monthly payment.

Brother Lee insisted, "Go ahead. I know it is right."

I was in deep turmoil because I had been counseled to do something I had never done before—to sign a contract without having the resources to meet the payments.

When Brother Lee sensed my feelings he sent me to President David O. McKay, who listened very carefully as I explained the circumstances.

He said, "You do this. It is the right thing." But he extended no resources to make the doing of it possible.

When I reported to Brother Lee he said, "That confirms what I have told you."

I was still not at peace, and then came the lesson. Elder Lee said, "Do you know what is wrong with you—you always want to see the end from the beginning."

I replied quietly that I wanted to see at least a few steps ahead. He answered by quoting from the sixth verse of the twelfth chapter of Ether: "Wherefore, dispute not because ye see not, for ye receive no witness until after the trial of your faith."

And then he added, "My boy, you must learn to walk to the edge of the light, and perhaps a few steps into the darkness, and you will find that the light will appear and move ahead of you."

And so it has—but only as we walked to the edge of the light.

About His Father's Business

LELAND E. ANDERSON

In the New Testament we read of Jesus as a boy, twelve years of age, speaking with the lawyers and doctors in the temple. They were astonished at his understanding and answers. Mary and Joseph too were amazed. When they asked him why he had dealt with them in such a manner, he replied, ". . . wist ye not that I must be about my Father's business?" (Luke 2:49.)

A forceful application of this event was related to me by my uncle, Joseph Johansen, from Mount Pleasant, Utah. He served in the mission field in Washington and Oregon, when Elder Melvin J. Ballard of the Council of the Twelve was president of that mission. This is his story as he related it to me:

"One day I received a telegram from Elder Ballard to meet

him at a certain station in a small town. There was pressing business to take care of in that part of the Lord's vineyard, and he wanted me with him. I went down to the depot on the appointed day, and as I sat waiting for the train to come in, the depot agent approached me and said: 'Why are you sitting here? Who are you waiting for?'

"I replied, 'I am waiting for the passenger train to pull in, because I am to meet a certain man who is on that train.'

" 'Well,' said the agent, 'then you may go home. This train is a through train, and under no condition will it ever stop at this station.'

" 'If you don't mind, will you pardon me if I sit here and watch the train go through town?' I replied.

" 'You may do so—that is your right,' the agent said."

On the train that day Elder Ballard asked the conductor if he would please stop the train at that particular station and let him off, because he had a very important meeting to hold. The conductor smiled and said, "You bet I will not stop this train. This is a through train. If I should stop it there, I might be the cause of a serious wreck. And besides, even if I didn't have a wreck, I would be fired from my job, because this train does not stop at that station." Elder Ballard thanked him as he continued on through the train.

Well, instead of going nonstop through the station, the train pulled onto the siding and stopped. For the first time in forty years, a too-lengthy freight train had pulled into the town half an hour before the passenger train was due. When it pulled onto the siding to let the passenger train pass, it proved to be too long for the siding.

Since the freight train could not be pulled off the main track, it backed up on the main track and waited for the passenger train to come in. Then the passenger train had to take the siding and wait while the freight train passed on through the town. During this time the conductor sought out Elder Ballard and said, "Mister, this has never happened before in forty years. May I ask, Who are you?"

Elder Ballard gave an answer similar to that of the Savior in the temple: "I am a minister of the gospel and I am about my Father's business. I knew this train would stop. I had faith that it would."

Confirmation that he was indeed on his Father's business came later that evening. Elder Ballard and the missionaries went out to an Indian reservation, where they spoke. As the apostle was speaking, the Indian chief came up from the audience, threw his arms around him, and said to his people: "This is the man I told you about that I saw in my dream. He has a book that purports to be the history of our people. Give heed to his teachings and counsel this night."

"*K*o E Maama E"

JOHN H. GROBERG

Editor's Note: The following experience is one of many tests of faith Elder John H. Groberg faced on his mission to the islands of Tonga during the 1950s.

On one occasion, we received word that a missionary was very ill on a somewhat distant island. The weather was threatening, but we felt responsible for the missionary's well-being. After prayer, we left to investigate the situation. Extra heavy seas slowed our progress, and it was late afternoon before we arrived. The missionary was indeed very ill. Fervent prayer was followed by a priesthood blessing, during which the impression came very strongly to get him back to the hospital on the main island, and to do it now!

The weather had deteriorated to the point of a small gale. The seas were raging, the clouds were thick, the wind was fierce, the hour was late, and the sun was sinking rapidly, betokening a long, black night ahead. But the impression was strong—"Get back now"—and we had learned to obey the all-important promptings of the Spirit.

Many on the island expressed concern, and we talked much about the darkness, the storm, and the formidable reef with its narrow opening to the harbor we would be attempting to gain. Some found reasons to stay behind. But soon eight persons—including an ill missionary, a very experienced captain, and a somewhat concerned district president, boarded the boat. The spiritually prompted voyage began.

No sooner had we committed ourselves to the open seas than the intensity of the storm seemed to increase sevenfold. The small gale became a major storm. As the sun sank below the horizon, bringing with it darkness and gloom, my spirit seemed to sink into the darkness of doubt and apprehension. The thick clouds and driving rain increased the blackness of our already dark universe. No stars. No moon. No rest. Only turmoil of sea, body, mind, and spirit. As we toiled on through that fearsome night, I found my spirit communing with the spirit of the father of an afflicted child in the New Testament, as he exclaimed, "Lord, I believe; help thou mine unbelief" (Mark 9:24). And the Lord did, and He does, and He will. That I know.

As we rolled and tossed closer and closer to the reef, all eyes searched for the light that marked the opening—the only entry to our home. Where was it? The blackness of the night seemed to increase; the fierceness of the raging elements seemed to know no bounds. The rain slashed at our faces and tore at our eyes—eyes vainly searching for that life-giving light.

Then I heard the chilling sound of waves crashing and chewing against the reef! It was close—too close. Where was the light? Unless we entered the opening exactly, we would be smashed against the reef, ripped and torn by that thousand-toothed monster. It seemed that all the elements were savagely bent on our destruction. Our eyes strained against the blackness, but we could not see the light.

Some began to whimper, others to moan and cry, and one or two even to scream in hysteria. At the height of this panic, when others were pleading to turn to the left or to the right, when the tumultuous elements all but forced us to abandon life and hope, I looked at the captain—and there I saw the face of calmness, the ageless face of wisdom and experience, as his eyes penetrated the darkness ahead. Quietly, his weather-roughened lips parted, and without moving his fixed gaze and just perceptibly shifting the wheel, he breathed those life-giving words, *"Ko e Maama e"* ("There is the light!")

I could not see the light, but the captain could see it, and I knew he could see it. Those eyes long experienced in ocean travel were not fooled by the madness of the storm, nor were they influenced by the pleadings of those of lesser experience to turn to the left or to the right. He calmly guided us forward. On one great swell, we were hurled through the opening and into calmer waters.

The roaring of the reef was now behind us. Its plan of destruction had been foiled. We were in the protected harbor. We were home. Then, and only then, did we see through the darkness that one small light—exactly where the captain had said it was. Had we waited until we ourselves could see the light, we would have been dashed to pieces, shredded on the reef of unbelief. But trusting in those experienced eyes, we lived.

That night I learned this great lesson: there are those who, through years of experience and training and by virtue of special divine callings, can see further, better, and more clearly than we can. They can and will save us in those situations where serious injury or death—both spiritual and physical—would be upon us before we ourselves could see clearly.

Hezekiah Mitchell:
"I Knew That Faith Must Prevail"

GARRETT H. GARFF

She's dead, Hezekiah. Our little girl is dead." Sarah Mitchell began to weep as she and her husband looked down at their two-year-old daughter, Elizabeth. The child was lying motionless on the bed. Her eyes stared straight ahead, and her face was a ghastly blue-gray color.

Little Elizabeth had recently been sick with the measles, but she had been showing signs of improvement. In fact, her parents thought she was just about over the illness. Then, during this night of July 10, 1848, Hezekiah and Sarah had been awakened to find that they now faced the terrible possibility that their daughter was dead.

However, drawing upon the strength of the Spirit, which had been his support on so many occasions, Hezekiah took his wife's trembling hand in his and said, "Be still, Sarah." He then looked more closely at Elizabeth to see if she was truly gone. He looked for a sign that she was breathing. There was none. He checked her pulse. There was nothing. He gently shook the little body. Again, there was no response.

He turned to his wife. "She is dead, but be still and I will lay hands on her and see what the Lord will do for us."

That Hezekiah Mitchell would express such faith in the power of the priesthood was not surprising. Though he had been a member of the Church for less than four years, he had already seen this power at work several times. As a branch president called to serve in the area of northern England where he lived, he had exercised the priesthood to heal sick persons and to cast out devils. Now he would call on that same power in behalf of his youngest daughter.

Laying his hands on her, in the name of Jesus Christ he commanded her to revive. But Elizabeth did not stir. There was still no sign of life in her.

Was it time to give up? Had death won and taken Hezekiah and Sarah's child away from them?

In Hezekiah's heart the answer was no. He would not give up. He had shown this kind of determination in a variety of ways since becoming a Latter-day Saint. His father was unhappy about Hezekiah's joining the Church and even told him he would never be welcome again in the family home. Yet Hezekiah continued to love his father and pleaded with him to open his heart to the restored gospel. In a letter to his father, Hezekiah testified boldly that the Church was true and that Joseph Smith was the Lord's prophet. "Father," he wrote, "it is not with any ill feelings which makes me talk so plain, but it is with a sincere desire for your salvation."

Just as he would not give up on his father, Hezekiah was not about to give up on Elizabeth. "I had faith still in the ordinance," he later wrote, "and I knew that faith must prevail." So once again he laid his hands on his daughter and blessed her in the Savior's name.

Suddenly Elizabeth gasped. And then she gasped again, and again. She was alive!

Before long she was breathing normally, and a healthy pink color returned to her face.

Rejoicing, Hezekiah and Sarah recognized the source of this great blessing and gave thanks to God. Such meekness was characteristic of Hezekiah, who once wrote, "My desire is that I may ever keep myself humble and teachable." And so it was that, in writing about the healing of his daughter, he declared, "To God be the glory."

Strong, Like the Pioneers

Bruce Newbold

Editor's Note: Bruce Newbold, an actor and writer, chronicled the events of those courageous modern-day pioneers who took part in the Sesquicentennial Mormon Trail Wagon Train of 1997. This is an excerpt from his collection.

In an effort to leave behind the trivial affairs that often clutter everyday life and to experience the hidden lessons of the trail, many came—though for a brief stay—to join the wagon train. But the reevaluation of life's perspectives that the trail selflessly reveals was sometimes taught in surprisingly unexpected ways. For example, joining the trek for a few days was the Kenneth and Pamela King family, from Twin Falls, Idaho. Their children included Aaron, 15; Kenny, 13; Megan, 10; Stuart, 9; Kandis, 4; and Jamison, who had just turned three. Their plans were to spend several days with the handcart company and share in an educational, pioneer experience. And that is precisely what they did.

On May 22nd, the wagon train traveled from North Paxton to Keystone, a distance of roughly sixteen miles. The Kings had struggled to keep up with the now seasoned walkers of the handcart company, and by the time the train pulled into camp, they were thoroughly tuckered. Not having eaten during the course of the morning, they were pretty anxious to participate when the lunch truck made its delivery rounds near 1:30 in the afternoon. Having spread a blanket near the carts, now enjoying the relief of removing boots from exhausted feet, Ken sent the hungry children to gather the necessary lunches for the family.

The teamsters had circled the wagons and had unhitched the horses and mules for the afternoon. This was the first time the King children had been around the wagons, and being interested in the horses, the older children stopped to help the younger ones pet the animals that were tied close by. Little Jamison, wearing his yellow jacket, was with them. When the children finished petting the horses, they made their way between the wagons to where the lunch sacks were being distributed.

"Make sure you make a wide berth around those horses, so you don't spook them," shouted Ken, as the six children disappeared around the side of a wagon.

Almost immediately thereafter, Ken saw a yellow blur out of the corner of his eye. It flew about six feet off the ground, then landed and rolled in the dirt some ten feet away from the wagon the children were next to.

Ken's first thought was, "How did Jamison climb up on that wagon without me seeing him, and then jump so far?"

As the little boy lay motionlessly in the dirt near one of the wagons, to their horror, both Ken and Pam realized that something critical must have happened. Crying out his name, they both hurried to him. As they rounded the side of the wagon, they noticed two mules which, from their vantage point on the blanket, had not been previously seen. One of the mules appeared agitated, prancing about, and pulling on its leadrope. It was then that they realized that Jamison had been kicked.

The little boy rolled onto his back. His right arm was extended straight up in the air. His right cheek and eye were puffy and swollen, and blood was coming from the same eye, his mouth, from under his chin, and by his ear. His face was blue. His left eye was open, but was rolling back inside his head, exposing mostly the white of his eye. He was trying to gasp for air, but was not breathing. Ken reached to lift him.

"Don't touch him! Don't touch him!"

Ken looked up. It was Cindy Wells, one of the company's EMTs, who was hurrying to the side of the child.

"But he's not breathing, and I've got to do something!"

"You don't know where he's been hurt. He may have hurt his neck. You've gotta keep him completely still."

She quickly knelt down, and after a few attempts of applying mouth-to-mouth resuscitation, tiny Jamison began to react. Though his breathing was chopping and sporadic, he was, at least, breathing.

He's leaving me, thought Ken, in the panic of the anxious moments. *I can just tell.* Jamison looked bad, and Ken feared the worst.

Nanc' Adams joined Cindy in administering medical attention the boy needed. An ambulance had been called immediately after the incident, and now they awaited its arrival.

Knowing the boy lacked a priesthood blessing, Ken called out to his friend, David Hunt, who stood nearby. "In my pack in the cart, I've got some consecrated oil. Go see if you can find it!"

As David raced away, Steve Sorensen, the executive secretary of the wagon train, held out a small bottle. "Here. I have some."

Being quickly invited to assist in giving Jamison a blessing, Steve anointed him, and Ken sealed the anointing, blessing the child that he would be calm, that he would be healed, and that no permanent damage would be realized through this incident.

Jamison's breathing was labored, at best, and the swelling on his face continued. His pupils were dilated. Wanting to make a more thorough examination, the EMTs Nanc' and Cindy removed his shirt. Though there was concern regarding some blue spots on his chest, stomach, and arms, it was at this time that Jamison rebelled at being undressed—the first good sign that he was coherent. But Pam gasped. She had seen splotches like that before, on the chest of their oldest boy, Aaron, when he had been run over by a car some twelve years ago. Aaron had sustained critical, life-threatening injuries, and among the outward manifestations of the internal damage, was a similar speckling on his skin.

Oh, Heavenly Father, don't take him from us, thought Ken, prayerfully and pleadingly, as he looked down on Jamison. *I'm not strong like the pioneers. I can't leave one on the plains. What a terrible thing it would do to the whole trek if a child dies. Please don't do that to these people. This is supposed to be a joyous occasion, not a sad experience.* The prayerful thoughts raced through Ken's mind.

When the ambulance arrived, they strapped Jamison to the stretcher. His parents' attempts to keep him still were fairly successful, but when he was placed upon the board, the little boy showed his spit and fire. With such a completely unfamiliar range of emotions and sensations running through his young system, he was at first angry, then submissive.

"Hold me, Mommy. Hold me, Mommy," he pleaded.

But she couldn't. She watched the ambulance doors close. That familiar expression of complete vulnerability passed between her and Ken; that expression that only reaffirms the fact that there are times when a Higher Power must reveal his will; that there is never a moment when we are not completely reliant upon him, and dependent upon his generous goodness.

With Ken accompanying Jamison in the back of the ambulance, the emergency crew sped away to the hospital in Ogallala. As they drove, further testing was done, vital signs were continuously monitored, and reports were transmitted to the doctors who awaited their arrival. The paramedics were convinced he had a shattered cheekbone, and were worried about internal bleeding in his head, chest and abdomen.

By the time they reached the hospital, the spots on his chest and arms were gone. Despite the improvement, they rushed him directly to the doctor who proceeded to examine him.

"Boy, the way you guys were describing him, I expected something much worse. This can't be the same boy you prepared me for."

"Well, he looks a lot better now than when we got to him at camp," responded the paramedic, in a pleasantly bewildered tone.

Indeed, it appeared that little Jamison was healing right before their eyes.

They took X rays. To their great relief and surprise, nothing was wrong. No fracture. No apparent internal bleeding. No need for stitches. The doctor simply cleaned him up and applied the small bandages on his chin and behind his ear. There was, although, the concern for a possible concussion, and with this in mind, Jamison was admitted for overnight observation.

No medication was prescribed, in view of the possible concussion, and Jamison was left to endure the aches of the accident. Complaining of pain in his cheek and neck, the unhappy little man tossed and turned on his bed, and for the next three hours told the doctor he "wanted to go home." The doctor, constantly amazed at how well he was doing, finally prescribed some Advil. Twenty minutes later, Jamison was feeling swell. The throbbing in his cheek had stopped, and he wanted out of that sterile environment! In compliance with Jamison's demonstrative requests, the doctor was "forced" to release the toddler that night at nine o'clock. Jamison was quickly taken to a nearby hotel and tucked into bed next to his mother.

After spending the night in Ogallala, the doctor advised them against putting Jamison quickly back on the wagon train. So, missing the day's travel from Keystone to Lemoyne, they rejoined the train as it set up camp on the afternoon of the 23rd. Much to their amazement, the first thing Jamison exclaimed when they got back to camp was, "Horsies! Horsies! I want to pet the horsies!"

Faith in the Tongan Islands

Eric Shumway

On Wednesday evening, March 15, 1961, we were gathered at the mission house in Neiafu with some of the Tongan missionaries of the Vava'u District. It was a kind of farewell get together and sleep-in since I was being transferred to Tongatapu the following day.

As we were talking, we heard a "caller" making his way through the village. In a loud voice he was warning the people that a hurricane would hit Vava'u at about five o'clock the following morning. The missionaries, most of whom were married and had small children, did not seem too concerned about it because the warnings of hurricanes came in March every year.

But at two o'clock the next morning the wind began to blow. By five it was very strong. Two missionaries came into the house from where they were sleeping and asked me to take them back to their villages in the mission car. I agreed, but when I opened the door to look out I saw the trees already coming down. The road was completely blocked and nothing could get through. I told the missionaries it might be safer if they would walk.

Before they got out of sight, the wind became really violent. This is when I realized we were in for a great hurricane, not just one that they have every year, but one which would make history.

We called all the people who lived nearby and invited them to go into the chapel. We didn't want anyone to stay in the older buildings, since they might collapse at any moment. I figured that two of the houses on the lot would probably be taken in the wind.

About nine o'clock, everything in the town began going up.

My Tongan companion and I stood out on the west side of the chapel (the wind was coming from the east) so we could see everything that went on in town. From where we stood, we could see houses being blown over and big trees torn up by their roots and thrown into the air. We could see the Wesleyan tabernacle, which is about a block from our chapel, being dismantled by invisible hands. We learned later that a man was crushed to death when the building collapsed. The Tongan Free Church tabernacle was also demolished.

At ten o'clock we estimated the wind to be about 150 miles an hour, an estimation that was later confirmed by the Tongan government.

Most of the houses which stood near our chapel were destroyed. The huge mango tree (a mango tree is comparable to the oak tree in America for strength) that stood across the street from our chapel was in ribbons. Large limbs, a foot in diameter, were torn off like match sticks and taken to the sea or dropped out in the road.

When the wind hit, we all noticed that Tonga Malohifo'ou was not at the chapel. Most of the Saints in the village and many nonmembers had come to our chapel for safety. As branch president, Brother Malohifo'ou should have been the first one there to help organize the "confusion." He didn't show up that morning or noon.

In America, President Malohifo'ou's little house would be called a wooden shack. Badly in need of repair, it was a fragile single frame structure built on four posts. It was far enough away from the chapel to make it very dangerous to go there in such wind.

That night he didn't show up at the chapel, and Friday morning he still wasn't there. About ten o'clock, the wind was still over a hundred miles an hour, but I couldn't restrain myself from trying to find him to see how his family was, for I loved them greatly. I asked Vili Pele to go with me and we ran to find President Malohifo'ou. When we reached his *api,* we were greatly surprised to see his house still standing, without any apparent damage, amid tons of debris. The Tongan Free Church tabernacle across the road had been razed. The large house that stood on the corner, very close to President Malohifo'ou's, had disappeared. The house on the other side of his *api* was completely demolished. The four vavae trees on his lot had fallen. But his little frame house still stood, and everything else on the lot was intact.

When we reached the house, I called to him to open the door. President Malohifo'ou had to brace himself against the door to let us in as the wind was still strong enough to take the door right off!

When we entered the house I thoroughly expected to see dead people. But his wife cheerfully called my name and invited us to sit down and eat some of the cold yam that they had eaten that morning. Again it surprised us that they had been able to build a fire and cook some food, for most of the people in Vava'u had been without food from Thursday through Friday morning.

The first thing I asked President Malohifo'ou was why he disregarded his position and did not go to the chapel with his wife. He didn't say anything, but just pointed to the little children on the floor. He told us he didn't dare go outside the house as one of them might have been killed. I told him I thought it would have been much better to try to go to the chapel than to stay there and be crushed to death in the house. He just smiled and said nothing.

When we persisted in asking him why he didn't make a break for the chapel, President Malohifo'ou began to weep and said, "Elder Shumway, I want you and Vili to come in here to this other room, and I'll tell you why I didn't go."

We went into the room and he said, "I've already told you why I didn't go. I was afraid to go outside. The wind hadn't really reached its peak, but I could hear the roof and feel the house shaking, as if it were ready to fall. I knew that if I stayed in the house I would die with my family, and if I went outside I'd die. At that time, I climbed up on this chair and I placed my hand right on the part of the roof I thought would go off first. I said, 'By the power of the priesthood which I hold, and in the name of Jesus Christ, I command you to stand solidly and completely throughout this storm.' I stopped the storm from this house, from this lot, and from these houses which stand on the lot."

President Malohifo'ou told us that after he had said these words, the house quit shaking, the roof quit rattling, the wind *seemed* to die down outside. But it hadn't. The wind *was* stopped from that little house, because he commanded it in the name of Jesus Christ and by the power of the priesthood!

For about five minutes Vili and I couldn't speak—couldn't say anything. Lumps were in my throat, and my heart was burning. We knew that the power of the Lord had been manifested.

The Little Blind Boy of Holland

OSBORNE J. P. WIDTSOE

I happened several years ago. The President of the Church Joseph F. Smith was visiting the Saints in all the branches of the Church in Europe. This particular month—the beautiful harvest month of August—he was to visit Rotterdam. Missionaries and Saints alike were anxious to see him, and were preparing for the great spiritual feast they should have when he came.

Little John, too, was waiting anxiously for the president to come. Not that little John could see him now. Unfortunately he could not. But Little John remembered with a thrill of pleasure that, two or three years before, he had been able to see as well as any of his playmates, and then he had loved to look upon the picture of the kind, sympathetic-looking president. Little John always imagined that he saw a halo of glory about the president's head.

But fortune had been unkind to Little John since those happy days—or so at least he thought. Although he was only eleven years old, he had now for several years suffered very much with his eyes. They were always inflamed, and there was always a terrible pain in them. The doctor had long ago made him discontinue school; so that now he stayed at home, wore a great bandage over his eyes, and spent most of his time thinking of how good the Lord had been to him at other times, and hoping that He would not forsake him now.

So Little John was waiting anxiously, too, for the President to come. The President was the greatest man on earth, thought Little John, and he wanted very much to hear him, at least, even if he could not see him.

The evening before the day on which the President was to visit the Saints of Rotterdam, Little John was unusually excited. He could speak of nothing but the President's visit, he could think of nothing else. He was literally possessed by uncontrollable enthusiasm.

"Oh, mama," he cried, "I'm so glad that I shall be able at least to hear the President. Just think, mama, he is the Prophet of God."

"Yes, my dear," answered his mama, "he is God's annointed prophet. I, too, am glad he is coming to visit us. It is almost as if the Lord himself were to come."

Little John was impressed. He remained quiet for a little while. He was in deep thought. It was almost the first time he had been quiet that day. By and by he spoke again.

"Mama, the prophet has the most power of any missionary on earth, hasn't he?"

"Yes, dear boy," said his mother, "he holds all the keys and authority that God gives to man. Why do you ask, my son?"

Little John was silent for another little while; then he said solemnly, fervently, "Mama, if you will take me with you to the meeting, and get the President to look into my eyes, I believe they will be healed."

"My dear boy," said his mother tenderly, "I know the President has power to heal you. But, my boy, the President is very busy just now. He has traveled far to visit us, and there are hundreds of people who want to see him. You are only a boy, my son, and we must not intrude nor force ourselves upon the President's notice."

Little John's spirits sank. Yes, he was only a boy; and the President, oh! he was such a great man. There would be so many at the meeting to see him, he would not notice the little boy.

"But mama," asked Little John after a while, "you will take me with you to the meeting, won't you?"

"Yes, my boy," said his mother.

"Then," said Little John, his spirits rising, "I shall hear the voice of the President—the Prophet; and oh! if he would only look into my eyes, I know they would be healed."

The next day Little John listened with rapture to the tones of the Prophet of God. Although the little boy could understand only what the interpreter said—for the President could not speak Dutch—yet he was warmed and thrilled by the kindly sounds of the President's voice.

When the service was over, the President went to the door to shake hands with the Saints as they passed out of the hall.

"Ah," thought Little John, "It is all over. But I have heard the Prophet's voice! I do wish I could meet him now and that he would look into my eyes."

Almost at that moment the mother said, "This is the President, Little John, he wants to shake hands with you."

A great warm hand took hold of Little John's and a kind voice greeted him tenderly. It was the President! Little John's heart beat so that it could almost be heard. Then the President's other hand lifted the bandage from Little John's eyes, and the President looked sympathetically into their sore and painful depths.

"The Lord bless you, my boy," the President said, placing a hand on Little John's head, "He will grant you the desire of your heart."

Now Little John was happy and contented indeed, and far more enthusiastic than ever before. He had heard the President's voice, and the President had looked into his eyes, and his eyes were feeling better, too.

When he reached home Little John could hardly contain himself. Suddenly he called out, "Oh, mama, my eyes are well; I can't feel any more pain at all. And oh, mama, I can see fine now, and far, too."

His mother ran to him, not knowing what to think. She tested him in every conceivable way; and, sure enough, he could see as well as ever he could.

By and by Little John spoke again, his voice almost choked with tears, "Mama," he asked, "The President's name is Joseph F. Smith, isn't it?"

"Yes, my dear," she answered. "He is a nephew of the Prophet Joseph."

"And I think he is a great prophet, too," said Little John. "He possesses just as much power and authority. Mama," he continued earnestly, "I shall pray for him always, for I know he is a true prophet of God."

Prayer

"Sh-h-h, Grandfather, I'm Listening"

Elaine Cannon

Some years ago, David Lawrence McKay shared a story about his grandchildren at bedtime. Grandpa was given the privilege of helping with prayers. The three-year-old knelt at Lawrence's knee and began the precious ritual. When the simple, earnest prayer was over, the child remained kneeling and silent. Unusual! Most scramble into life again with demands for stuffed toys, bedtime stories, drinks of water, and yet another goodnight kiss. Not this one. The silence persisted until Grandpa questioned why the child didn't pop into bed.

"Sh-h-h, Grandfather. I am listening!"

Ah-ah! And shouldn't listening be part of all communication? Particularly with Heavenly Father. Such lessons the little ones can teach.

Sept 13, 2004

Beth's Birthday Present

ALLAN K. BURGESS

When Beth was ten years old, her Primary teacher taught her class that Heavenly Father would answer their prayers if they asked in faith and if what they desired was right for them. Beth was the only active member of the Church in her family, and this lesson so inspired her that, upon arriving home, she immediately went to her room and began to pray. She said, "Heavenly Father, you know my father is a good man and a good father, but he never goes to church—not even when I have a part on the program. Oh, Heavenly Father, please touch my father's heart so he will have the desire to go to church so we can become an eternal family."

Several times every day for six years Beth pleaded with the Lord in behalf of her father. Many times during these six years she would break down and cry as she poured out her soul to God. Some people may have given up after just a few months—let alone six years—but Beth's faith never faltered.

Three or four days before her sixteenth birthday, the family was sitting around the breakfast table. Little did Beth know that her faithful prayers were about to be answered. Her father asked her what she would like for her birthday. He was a well-to-do building contractor and had purchased Beth's sister a new car for her sixteenth birthday just a year before. Beth's father told her that she could have anything she wanted and that money was no problem.

Beth was about ready to suggest a new car when the Holy Ghost spoke to her and said, "Beth, here is your chance! Here is what you have been hoping and praying for all of these years!" The Spirit then told her what to ask for.

When I first heard this story I thought she was going to ask her dad to start attending church, but this was not the case. God had something much more powerful than this in mind— something that would change Beth's dad forever.

After pausing a few seconds, Beth said, "Dad, there is one thing I would like to have more than anything else in this world, and it won't cost you one penny."

This really excited her father, and he wanted to know what this marvelous thing was that would not cost him anything. Beth said she would not tell him until he promised her that he would give it to her. Her father did not feel this was fair, and the rest of the family took his side, but she stood firm.

Seeing that she was not going to give in, her father finally said, "All right, I promise!"

Beth said, "Dad, the one thing I want more than anything else in this world is that we kneel down every morning to-gether as a family in family prayer." Her father later said it was like someone dropped a ton of bricks on him—he just sat there stunned. It was a request he had least expected but knew he must fulfill in order to maintain his integrity with Beth.

The next morning, true to his word, the father called the family together for family prayer. He called upon Beth to give the prayer because she was the only one in the family who was active. Beth gave the prayer every morning for the first week. After about a week, the mother said that she would be willing to take a turn, and it wasn't long until Beth's older sister began to pray. Soon her two little brothers were praying also. As a matter of fact, everyone in the family was praying except the father—the one who had been the center of Beth's prayers for six years.

After about a month, as the family knelt for prayer one morning there was a pause for a moment, and then the father said, "I guess it's about my turn to pray." Beth said as her father began to pray, tears welled up in her eyes and rolled down her cheeks. She felt that she was hearing the most humble and beautiful prayer that had ever been expressed by the lips of a mortal man. It was wonderful! It was the first time she had ever heard her father pray, and the spiritual effect it had upon the whole family was overwhelming. When the prayer was over, the whole family came together in one big hug of emotion and wept in gratitude for the great blessing that had come into their home.

This was the beginning of activity for Beth's family, and it was not long until they were all going to church together. Beth spent her seventeenth birthday in the Salt Lake Temple, kneeling at a holy altar with her family as they made eternal covenants together.

$\mathcal{T}$he Lord's Wind

JOHN H. GROBERG

Editor's Note: The following is one of many faith-promoting experiences Elder John H. Groberg was privileged to receive on his mission to the islands of Tonga during the 1950s.

F inding someone willing to listen to the discussions was like finding a piece of gold, especially if a member had referred them. One day we received such a referral. We were told that if we would be at a certain harbor on a particular island when the sun set the next day, a family would meet us there and listen to the discussions.

What joy such news gives to missionaries! I quickly found four members who were experienced sailors to take me to the island.

Early the next morning, after prayer, the five of us started out in our sailboat. There was a nice breeze, and we moved swiftly along the coast, through the opening in the reef, and out into the wide expanse of the open ocean. We made good progress for a few hours. Then as the sun climbed higher in the sky and the boat got farther from land, the wind played out and soon quit completely, leaving us bobbing aimlessly on a smooth sea.

Those familiar with sailing know that to get anywhere, you must have wind. Sometimes there are good breezes without storms and heavy seas, but often they go together. An experienced sailor does not fear storms or heavy seas, for they contain the lifeblood of sailing—wind. What experienced sailors fear is no wind, or being becalmed!

Time passed and the sun got higher, the sea calmer. Nothing moved. We soon realized that unless something changed, we would not arrive at our appointment by sundown. I suggested that we pray and plead again with the Lord to send some wind so we could get to the harbor. What more righteous desire could a group of men have? We wanted to get to a family to teach the gospel. I offered a prayer. When I finished, things seemed calmer than ever. When it was obvious nothing was happening, I said, "Okay, which one of you is like Jonah? Who lacks faith? We'll throw you overboard so the Lord can send the wind and we can get on with our journey." No one would admit to being like Jonah, so we just drifted.

Then one of the older men suggested that everyone kneel and all unite their faith and prayers, each one offering a silent prayer at the same time, which we did. There was great struggling of spirit, but when the last person opened his eyes, nothing! No movement at all. The sails hung limp and listless. Even the slight ripple of the ocean against the side of the boat had ceased. The ocean seemed like a sea of glass.

Time was moving, and we were getting desperate. Then this same older man suggested that everyone kneel again in prayer, and each person in turn offer a vocal prayer for the whole group. Many beautiful, pleading, faithful prayers ascended to heaven. But when the last one finished and everyone opened their eyes, the sun was still burning down with greater intensity than before. The ocean was like a giant mirror. It was almost as though Satan was laughing, saying, "See, you can't go anywhere. There is no wind. You are in my power."

I thought, "There is a family at the harbor that wants to hear the gospel. We are here and we want to teach them. The Lord controls the elements. All that stands between getting the family and us together is a little wind. Why won't the Lord send it? It's a righteous desire."

As I was thinking, I noticed this faithful older man move to the rear of the boat. I watched as he unlashed the tiny lifeboat, placed two oars with pins into their places, and carefully lowered the lifeboat over the side.

Then the old man looked at me and softly said, "Get in."

I answered, "What are you doing? There is hardly room for two people in that tiny thing!"

The old man responded, "Don't waste any time or effort. Just get in. I am going to row you to shore, and we need to leave right now to make it by sundown."

I looked at him incredulously, "Row me *where?*"

"To the family that wants to hear the gospel. We have an assignment from the Lord. Get in."

I was dumbfounded. It was miles and miles to shore. The sun was hot and this man was old. But as I looked into the face of that faithful brother, I sensed an intensity in his gaze, an iron will in his very being and a fixed determination in his voice as he said, "Before the sun sets this day, you will be teaching the gospel and bearing testimony to a family who wants to listen."

I objected, "Look, you're over three times my age. If we're going to do it this way, fine, but let me row."

With that same look of determination and faith-induced will, the old man replied, "No. Leave it to me. Get in the boat. Don't waste time talking or moving unnecessarily. Let's go!" We got into the boat with me in the front and the old man in the middle with his feet stretching to the rear of the boat, his back to me.

The glazed surface of the ocean was disturbed at the intrusion of this small boat and seemed to complain, "This is my territory. Stay out." Not a wisp of air stirred, not a sound was heard except the creaking of oars and the rattling of pins as the small craft began to move away from the side of the sailboat.

The old man bent his back and began to row—dip, pull, lift, dip, pull, lift. Each dip of the oar seemed to break the resolve of the mirrorlike ocean. Each pull of the oar moved the tiny skiff forward, separating the glassy seas to make way for the Lord's messenger.

Dip. Pull. Lift. The old man did not look up, rest, or talk. But hour after hour he rowed and rowed and rowed. The muscles of his back and arms, strengthened by faith and moved by unalterable determination, flexed in a marvelous cadence like a fine-tuned watch. We moved quietly, relentlessly toward an inevitable destiny. The old man concentrated his efforts and energy on fulfilling the calling he had from the Lord—to get the missionary to the family that wanted to hear the gospel. He was the Lord's wind that day.

Just as the sun dipped into the ocean, the skiff touched the shore of the harbor. A family was waiting. The old man spoke for the first time in hours and said, "Go. Teach them the truth. I'll wait here."

I waded ashore, met the family, went to their home, and taught them the gospel. As I bore testimony of the power of God in this Church, my mind seemed to see an old man rowing to a distant harbor and patiently waiting there. I testified with a fervor as great as any I have ever felt that God does give power to men to do His will if they have faith in Him. I said, "When we exercise faith in the Lord Jesus Christ, we can do things we could not otherwise do. When our hearts are determined to do right, the Lord gives us the power to do so."

The family believed and eventually was baptized.

In the annals of Church history, few will be aware of this small incident. Hardly anyone will know about this insignificant island, the family who waited, or the obscure, old man who never once complained of fatigue, aching arms, a painful back, or a hurting body. He never talked about thirst, the scorching sun, or the heat of the day as he relentlessly rowed uncomplainingly hour upon hour and only referred to the privilege of being God's agent in bringing a missionary to teach the truth to those who desired to hear. But God knows! He gave him the strength to be His wind that day, and He will give us the strength to be His wind when necessary.

"*I* Know He Won't Catch Anything"

BOYD K. PACKER

Here is a lesson drawn from a little girl who reported to her mother that her brother was setting traps for birds. She didn't like it at all.

"He won't catch any birds in his trap, will he, Mother?" she asked. "I have prayed about it and asked Heavenly Father to protect the birds. He won't catch anything, will he, Mother?" Becoming more positive, she said, "I *know* he won't catch anything, because I have prayed about it."

The mother asked, "How can you be sure he won't catch anything?"

Then came a meaningful addition: "He won't catch anything because, after I said my prayers, I went out and kicked that old trap all to pieces."

I think no editorializing on that is necessary.

A Message from the Heart

C. Steven Hatch

Our eldest daughter, Sharon, recently returned from her mission to France and Belgium, had decided to spend the summer in Anchorage, Alaska, with her missionary companion, Cindy Phillips. She had obtained a position as a clerk at the Travelodge in Anchorage, and was apparently having a wonderful summer, for she decided to delay her return home to Provo and her studies in the honors program at BYU until the following spring semester.

On September 17, I received a phone call from Alaska informing me that Sharon and a friend had been on a short plane trip and had failed to return. A storm had come up and the possibility of their being down somewhere safe was being held out.

I was in hopes that I would shortly receive another phone call telling me that all was well—that Sharon and her friend had been found and had not sustained any injuries, that I could spare my wife and the younger children the anxiety that I was experiencing. I confided the experience and my concern only to my son Steven, who had also filled a mission in France.

It took until the next day about 11:00 p.m. for another telephone communication. At that time, Cindy told me that search parties had been out all that day, but had not been able to identify any downed aircraft or wreckage as the weather was so bad. The search had ended for the day due to darkness, but the search would be resumed again the following morning. As it was also possible that the plane could have been safely down and Sharon would not have been able to contact Cindy to assure her of her safety because communications are so poor in the remote areas of Alaska, the possibility that Sharon was alive and well was very real.

By this time I felt that I had to inform my wife and the rest of the family of our concern for Sharon. We united in fasting and prayer and during the following day we had the opportunity to review the patriarchal blessing which Brother Sandgrin had given Sharon before she had gone to Alaska. In the blessings, she was promised that she would be sealed in the temple to a faithful companion. From this we took considerable reassurance that all *had* to be well with Sharon.

About nine o'clock that evening, we received another phone call from Anchorage, this time with Cindy's father, Brother Phillips, on the line informing us that the wreckage of the plane had been sighted and Sharon had been killed.

We were stunned, grief-stricken, tearful and yet somewhat composed at this tragic news; that is, except for our fourteen-year-old daughter Mary Ellen, who simply could not accept the reality of Sharon's death. She insisted that Sharon was too young and too good to have been taken. She began pleading with me to please contact President Harold B. Lee or one of the apostles to inquire if it really was the will of the Lord that Sharon's life be cut so short, and if not, that we ask them to command Sharon to return!

In my desire to comfort my grieving daughter, I expressed to her my feelings that in the plan of things all was well with Sharon, and that Sharon was one of those choice few that were well prepared for this step in our progression. With that assurance, Mary Ellen seemed quieter. She then went to her room and unknown to us, wrote the following letter:

"Dear President Lee,

"I don't want to take up your valuable time, but I need to ask a favor, if you please would.

"This Thursday, my sister was found dead in an airplane out of Anchorage, Alaska. She had been missing since Tuesday. All our family had fasted and prayed for her. My father says that it is the Lord's will, and I would like to believe him, but she was so young and good. I've heard that sometimes people die when they still have work to do here.

"What I would like to ask of you is, if you would pray, or have some other General Authority pray, to see if this is the right thing, or if she could be commanded to return. Whatever you tell me I would try to believe because you are a prophet of God.

"Thank you for taking the time to read this.

"Love,

"Mary Ellen Hatch"

Mary Ellen was calmer as she rejoined the family, and we all joined hands and kneeled about our king-sized bed for family prayers that night.

The next day we began to receive telephone calls from friends who wished to express their love and sympathy to us as a family, which was very comforting. Later that evening, about nine o'clock, the telephone rang. When I answered, the voice on the other end said, "This is Harold B. Lee."

I recovered from my surprise soon enough to summon the other members of the family, who hurried to the four telephones we have at the house. With two of us at each phone, we listened as President Lee expressed his love and his recognition of how we felt. He explained that he too had very suddenly lost his own precious daughter, who had also lived in Provo. This had come as a terrible shock to him, and again he reminded us that he knew of our feelings. He went on to point out to us that the blessings which are promised to the faithful will not be curtailed because of the short span of mortality. President Lee then assured us that Sharon's promised blessings would not be curtailed and that *all* of them would be fulfilled. He reminded us that birth into this life was not the beginning nor death the end of life in the eternities, and that all the blessings to the faithful would be fulfilled. He again expressed his love for us and gave us the assurance that all was indeed well with Sharon.

As President Lee hung up the phone, Mary Ellen ran into the kitchen, threw her arms around me, and said, "Daddy, that's all I needed. He answered every question I had asked him in my letter!"

We were not aware that Mary Ellen had written to the prophet. When we questioned her about it, she went to her room and returned with the letter. "I didn't mail the letter, Daddy," she said. "He must have heard the message from my heart!"

George Washington Prays at Valley Forge

Mason Weems

Editor's Note: Regarding this story, William J. Bennett has written: "Though some have disputed the accuracy of Washington biographer Mason Weems's depiction of Washington's praying at Valley Forge, many of Washington's fellow officers, such as Alexander Hamilton, reported that they often saw General Washington at prayer" (OUR SACRED HONOR [New York: Simon and Schuster, 1997], p. 372).

In the winter of '77, while Washington, with the American army, lay encamped at Valley Forge, a certain good old friend, of the respectable family and name of Potts, if I mistake not, had occasion to pass through the woods near head quarters. Treading in his way along the venerable grove, suddenly he heard the sound of a human voice, which, as he advanced, increased on his ear; and at length became like the voice of one speaking much in earnest. As he approached the spot with a cautious step, whom should he behold, in a dark natural bower of ancient oaks, but the commander in chief of the American armies on his knees at prayer! Motionless with surprise, friend Potts continued on the place till the general, having ended his devotions, arose; and, with a countenance of angelic serenity, retired to headquarters. Friend Potts then went home, and on entering his parlour called out to his wife, "Sarah! my dear Sarah! all's well! all's well! George Washington will yet prevail!"

"What's the matter, Isaac?" replied she, "thee seems moved."

"Well, if I seem moved, 'tis no more than what I really am. I have this day seen what I never expected. Thee knows that I always thought that the sword and the gospel were utterly inconsistent; and that no man could be a soldier and a christian at the same time. But George Washington has this day convinced me of my mistake."

He then related what he had seen, and concluded with this prophetical remark—"If George Washington be not a man of God, I am greatly deceived—and still more shall I be deceived, if God do not, through him, work out a great salvation for America."

She Expected an Answer

Sarah H. Bradford

Editor's Note: Harriet Tubman, a former slave who led a heroic struggle for her people in the Civil War, was more successful than any other person of her time in liberating African-Americans from slavery.

O
n one of her journeys to the North, as she was piloting a company of refugees, Harriet came, just as morning broke, to a town, where a colored man had lived whose house had been one of her stations of the under-ground, or unseen railroad. They reached the house, and leaving her party huddled together in the middle of the street, in a pouring rain, Harriet went to the door, and gave the peculiar rap which was her customary signal to her friends. There was not the usual ready response, and she was obliged to repeat the signal several times. At length a window was raised, and the head of a *white man* appeared, with the gruff question, "Who are you?" and "What do you want?" Harriet asked after her friend, and was told that he had been obliged to leave for "harboring niggers."

Here was an unforeseen trouble; day was breaking, and daylight was the enemy of the hunted and flying fugitives. Their faithful leader stood one moment in the street, and in that moment she had flashed a message quicker than that of the telegraph to her unseen Protector, and the answer came as quickly; in a suggestion to her of an almost forgotten place of refuge. Outside of the town there was a little island in a swamp, where the grass grew tall and rank, and where no human being could be suspected of seeking a hiding place. To this spot she conducted her party; she waded the swamp, carrying in a basket two well-drugged babies (these were a pair of little twins, whom I have since seen well grown young women), and the rest of the company following. She ordered them to lie down in the tall, wet grass, and here she prayed again, and waited for deliverance. The poor creatures were all cold, and wet, and hungry, and Harriet did not dare to leave them to get supplies; for no doubt the man at whose house she had knocked, had given the alarm in the town; and officers might be on the watch for them. They were truly in a wretched condition, but Harriet's faith never wavered, her silent prayer still ascended, and she confidently expected help from some quarter or other.

It was after dusk when a man came slowly walking along the solid pathway on the edge of the swamp. He was clad in the garb of a Quaker; and proved to be a "friend" in need and indeed; he seemed to be talking to himself, but ears quickened by sharp practice caught the words he was saying:

"My wagon stands in the barn-yard of the next farm across the way. The horse is in the stable; the harness hangs on a nail." And the man was gone. Night fell, and Harriet stole forth to the place designated. Not only a wagon, but a wagon well provisioned stood in the yard; and before many minutes the party were rescued from their wretched position, and were on their way rejoicing, to the next town. Here dwelt a Quaker whom Harriet knew, and he readily took charge of the horse and wagon, and no doubt returned them to their owner. How the good man who thus came to their rescue had received any intimation of their being in the neighborhood Harriet never knew. But these sudden deliverances never seemed to strike her as at all strange or mysterious; her prayer was the prayer of faith, and she *expected* an answer.

"Pray for Her"

ANITA R. CANFIELD

I had to fly to Mexico City one Thursday evening to inspect a project site under my design direction. The clients were leaving on Saturday for a two-month tour of their factories in Europe and the Orient, and there were dozens of questions to be resolved with them and the contractors that Friday. It had been a last minute request on their part, and my trip was going to be an overnight, but very intense, visit.

I arrived at the hotel around midnight and went immediately to sleep. Around three o'clock in the morning I was awakened by an excruciating, stabbing pain in my mouth with what would be classified as an extreme dental emergency.

My husband had done some dental work on me earlier in the week in preparation for further work the next week. I was in excruciating pain. I didn't know what to do. A million dollars of decisions were resting on me the next day. I had to be clear-minded and alert, especially with the language barrier; my Spanish is only adequate and requires great concentration on my part.

My first thought was to call my husband and get the name of a drug that would stop the pain. Then I worried that it wouldn't be the same dosage or type in Mexico. Then I wondered if the concierge would be able to find someone at three o'clock in the morning to even obtain it. And then, with complete realization, it occurred to me that any drug strong enough to knock out this pain would completely knock me out, and I would be useless the next day. I didn't know what to do.

Then came the distinct and clear message: "You have faith. You know what to do."

I climbed out of bed, knelt in prayer, and told the Lord of my situation and all that had concerned me, and asked him to

134

please take away the pain long enough for me to complete my work the next day. Before I said "in the name of Jesus Christ, amen," the pain vanished. Instantly, in a moment, it was gone. I thanked him and went back to sleep.

The next day I was able to answer the questions, make urgent and very critical decisions, and finish on time to catch my flight home. By the time I was in customs in Los Angeles, the pain was returning. When I landed in Las Vegas several hours later, I had another full-blown dental emergency!

But this is not the whole story. Two days later was fast Sunday. In our monthly family testimony meeting I told of my experience and my witness of the power of faith and prayer.

My fifteen-year-old son grew amazed. I could see his countenance change. When I finished speaking he asked, "Mom, was this Thursday night?"

"Yes," I said.

"And was it about two o'clock in the morning?"

I thought about that, it was three o'clock in Mexico, but with the hour time change I told him it was two o'clock in Las Vegas.

Suddenly he was filled with emotion and told me the beginning of the story. He had been awakened at two o'clock in the morning that night with a voice that said, "Your mother is in trouble, pray for her." He had slipped out of bed, and on his knees, with real intent, had said, "Heavenly Father, my mom has faith. Tell her what to do."

The Lord heard his prayer and reminded his mother of her faith and that she knew what to do.

Humility
and
Obedience

$\mathscr{A}$ Different Kind of Courage

☆Wayne B. Lynn

It happened in a rather common place, for that seems to be where most heroic deeds happen. It happened in a stake priesthood meeting on a hot July afternoon. The chapel was filled to overflowing, and the partition doors leading into the cultural hall had been opened to accommodate the large body of the priesthood. A special spirit seemed to be with us that day as our beloved stake president presided over us and conducted the affairs of the stake.

One lad who appeared to be about the age of a priest sat in a rather conspicuous place on the stand near the stake presidency. I had correctly guessed that he was to take part on the program, and I sympathized with his contained nervousness.

Soon the president announced the young man as the next speaker. He arose quietly and walked the short distance to the stand. His outward composure was calm, but my vantage point near the front of the room permitted me a view of the quivering hands that told of the fear to be conquered.

Taking a deep breath, he began to speak. It was quickly obvious that he had spent much time in preparation. An occasional glance at his notes was all that was required. I began to relax a little in my apprehension for him, but then I noticed that his speech was beginning to come faster and faster. Words were coming so fast that they were being repeated unnecessarily. In the middle of his next sentence he began to stammer. This increased his nervousness to the degree that his stammering continued, making him entirely speechless.

A sympathetic silence filled the room. I longed to reassure him or indicate in some way my sympathy and understanding, but, like the others, I waited. I waited for him to surrender and perhaps try again another day.

I could see the youth waging an inward battle as he stood there before us. Then it happened. He squared his shoulders and girded himself to the task, uttering, as nearly as I can recall, these words: "Brethren, I ask for an interest in your faith and prayers that I might have sureness of speech."

It was as if I had seen a miracle. He began again to speak, slowly, deliberately, but with sureness and conviction. His young voice rang out in a message that thrilled my soul. It is not his words I remember, but stamped indelibly upon my memory is the message of the boy himself.

Somehow, I will never feel the same again when I am called upon to perform a difficult task. Perhaps I can take a few steps up the same trail blazed by this brave young man, for he had climbed the mount of moral courage and stood unflinching upon its precipice.

His talk was soon completed. He gathered his notes and turned away from the stand, and for a moment I saw more than a young man in a white shirt. I saw a knight in shining armor with a sword at his side and a token of victory in his hand. The words of a song surged into my consciousness so strongly that they seemed to be crying out to be heard: "Behold! A royal army, with banner, sword, and shield, is marching forth to conquer on life's great battlefield. Its ranks are filled with soldiers, united, bold, and strong, who follow their Commander and sing their joyful song: Victory, victory"! ("Behold! A Royal Army," *Hymns,* no. 251.)

"Only God Gives A's"

Brett G. London

An institute instructor once told me that college students generally receive higher grades after completing a mission. I believed him. But that was before my mission—before I returned to college and attended an English class.

Since I was an English major, the most important class of the semester was "Analysis of Literary Forms." I needed straight A's in the final three years of college in order to be accepted by a law school I hoped to attend. Unfortunately, the professor of the class was on a personal crusade to combat grade inflation.

Adding to my anxiety was the professor's anti-religious cynicism. On the first day of class he boasted that his greatest accomplishment had been flunking a member of a religious order for cheating. Before long I realized that I was the only Mormon in a class full of agnostics.

Our first assignment was an analysis of a short story. I spent two weeks brainstorming, outlining, writing, and rewriting until I felt assured of an A. When my paper was returned, I was sickened to see the grade was a C.

I approached the professor after class and asked what was required in order to receive an A. He responded with a sneer, "Only God gives A's." Seeing that I wasn't amused, he explained that he would award an A only if he felt the paper was worthy of publication. My grade on the next assignment was critical. This time we had only one week in which to analyze a novel, and the professor couldn't have picked a worse week. Monday night was a special family home evening. I spent Tuesday night completing my home teaching. On Wednesday, I was assigned to conduct a Young Adult activity. Thursday was quarterly stake priesthood meeting, and I had been asked to speak.

On Friday I showed a friend from the mission field the sights of southern California. Saturday, I did yardwork for an incapacitated family. That evening, I attended a baptism and confirmation of a close friend.

I had done absolutely nothing on the paper when Sunday arrived. The paper was due Monday morning. Since it was fast Sunday, I had no commitments that afternoon or evening. I was tempted to do my homework, rationalizing that I had been doing the Lord's work the rest of the week. This was a good example of the ox in the mire, I thought. Then I remembered that I had promised Heavenly Father that I would never do schoolwork on the Sabbath. Since I had made that personal promise to the Lord, I called upon him for strength to keep my promise.

When I awakened Monday morning, only a couple of hours remained until the deadline. I spent half of the time brainstorming and the other half typing a single draft. I had no time for an outline, revision, or corrections.

I handed in the essay, fully expecting to fail the assignment. But I had done the best I could do and still keep my promise to the Lord.

When I entered class a week later, the essays were stacked on the professor's desk. As usual, he waited until the end of class to return them. This time I was willing to wait, especially since I had no desire ever to see my paper again.

The class came to a close. The professor picked up the papers. Instead of hurriedly passing them down the rows, he just stood there, looking down at the stack. Then he began flipping through the pages of the paper on top. He slowly lifted his eyes to look at the class, hesitated for a moment, and said softly, "Class, I suppose I have a reputation for being a hard grader. Well, I want you to know that today, for the first time in my teaching career, I have awarded a student an A-plus." It was my paper.

Perhaps the professor was right after all when he said, "Only God gives A's."

Humility Is Royalty Without a Crown

SPENCER W. KIMBALL

Humility is royalty without a crown,
Greatness in plain clothes,
Erudition without decoration,
Wealth without display,
Power without scepter or force,
Position demanding no preferential rights,
Greatness sitting in the congregation,
Prayer in closets and not in corners of the street,
Fasting in secret without publication,
Stalwartness without a label,
Supplication upon its knees,
Divinity riding an ass.

Lesson at the Gas Pump

RANDAL A. WRIGHT

It had been a good day at the LDS institute where I taught. Classes went well and the students seemed interested in the gospel principles discussed. It was one of those days that I realized just how many blessings I had been given in life.

While driving home that evening I glanced down at the dash and noticed the gas gauge was past empty. Luckily a self-serve gas station was just ahead, so I pulled in and began to fill the gas tank. That was a close call! While pumping the gas I continued reflecting on my blessings.

After a few moments an old, dilapidated car pulled up at another set of pumps. The driver looked very rough, and I began counting my blessings even more. His hair was long; he had a straggly beard and a cigarette in his mouth. As he got out of his car, I noticed that his clothes were tattered and in sad shape. I was thankful for my nice dark suit. *Poor guy,* I thought. *He doesn't have a chance in life!*

I finished pumping the gas and walked up to pay the cashier. Reaching into my pocket, I found that I had a slight problem—no money! After checking all my pockets, I told the cashier I'd be right back, that I needed to run to the car to get some money.

I searched everywhere in the car, but found nothing. I had no choice but to go back to the cashier. I would explain that my home was only about a mile and a half away, and that I'd be right back with the money.

To say that I was frustrated and irritated as I walked back toward the building would be an understatement. To make things worse, the ragged young man with the battered car passed by me returning to his car and said, "Don't worry about it." I thought, *Same to you, buddy,* although I had no idea what he was talking about.

When I got to the cashier and explained my predicament, she informed me that the young man saw what was happening and paid my bill. He told her to tell me not to worry about it. I couldn't believe it. I quickly ran over to his car and told him that I really appreciated what he'd done for me, but that I lived close by and would be right back with the money.

He just smiled and said, "Don't worry about it. I know what it's like to be broke." Then he drove off, leaving me standing there feeling like a total idiot.

Later I conjured up a mental picture of what it might be like at the final judgment. I could just see this young man being called before the bar and asked a few questions. "Did you smoke while you lived on earth?"

"Yes," came his reply.

"Did you realize that tobacco was not good for the body?"

He said he didn't realize it when he started but then got hooked.

"I'm sorry. That is a minus five on your test of life." The young man was then asked, "Did you love your neighbor and try to help those in need?"

He answered that he did try to do that.

I yelled out that he had helped me at the gas station. I could just hear the eternal judge saying, "Plus fifty! You took care of the most important things in life."

Then I imagined myself being called before the bar. I was still in my nice dark suit. My first imagined question was, "Did you smoke while you lived on earth?"

Proudly I quoted D&C 89:8: "Tobacco is not for the body."

"Good, that's a plus five in the test of life." Then I was asked, "Did you love your neighbor and try to help those in need? Or did you think you were better than they are because of all the blessings you were given?"

What could I say?

Then I could hear the words, "Minus fifty! You forgot to take care of the most important things in life."

I could just imagine the young man saying to me, "Don't worry about it. Maybe the telestial kingdom won't be that bad!"

Of course, I was just imagining the judgment bar scene. I don't pretend to know the specifics of how the judgment will occur or what questions will be asked. But when I get a little prideful about all I have been blessed with, or when I find myself judging others who have less or appear unworthy, I remember the important lesson I learned at the gas pump, and realize just how far I still have to go.

The Long Walk

MARION D. HANKS

I was twelve years old and a Tenderfoot Scout when I experienced my first overnight excursion away from home. I was excited, and I was frightened; we all were.

The group of boys who lined up with their gear on the lawn of the old Nineteenth Ward building in Salt Lake Stake were variously equipped for the planned adventure to Lake Blanche in the high mountains to the south and east of us. Some had elaborate and expensive sleeping bags and pack frames, and some had bedrolls attached to old army knapsacks. I was in between, having the use of a homemade bag fashioned by my brother-in-law, together with the pack frame he had built on which the bag and contents would be lashed.

All of us had been told to lay out our equipment for inspection by the man in charge, and we each fearfully waited by our stuff as the examiner approached. No marine trainee facing his drill instructor could have been more apprehensive.

The man passed down the line rather quickly, commenting on this item or that boy's pack, directing the abandonment of this extra baggage, sending one boy home to his mother with the three clean sheets she had sent along for his big trip.

I was last in line and thus nearest home, since our little house lay just alongside the old Relief Society building that separated us from the chapel. There was a narrow alley between the chapel and that building, and at the end of it a wall which formed the east border of our yard.

Being closest to home might have been an indicator of my frame of mind, because I was not altogether sold on this adventure and I was a bit apprehensive about the equipment I had borrowed, having been admonished carefully to keep it very clean and in absolute good repair.

By the time the inspector reached me, many foolish questions had been asked and answered, with increasing impatience on his part, I suspect, so that the man as he faced me had become a bit short on goodwill. He was, in fact, quite a dynamic person of whom I was somewhat afraid, though he had always been appropriately dignified in his calling and never had been anything but kind to me.

This day, under the circumstances and with the provocation of so much juvenile incompetency, he reached the end of his rope. Observing the number of items I was carrying which seemed to him superfluous for the high mountains and which he felt should not be carried in my pack, he sternly directed me to remove them and take them home to my mother. He seemed to dwell a bit sarcastically upon the pronunciation of my first name, about which my life on the west side of town by the railroad tracks had made me a bit touchy, if not defensive.

When he seemed to be making fun of me, the other boys up the line, having had their turn, snickered or broke into open laughter. Everybody but I thought it was funny. When he had left me and returned up the line to begin to herd the crowd onto the trucks which were to transport us, I made my gesture of protest. Not having anything else to do that I could think of, I just bent over, picked up the pack frame in one hand and the two ends of the sleeping bag on which my gear was resting in the other, and walked up the alley, dragging it all behind me. When I reached the wall I dropped over, retrieved the equipment, and dragged it all behind the coal shed which was separated by a few feet from our house. Then I sat down on the ground under the basketball hoop on the back of the coal shed and suffered the pains and anguish of the damned—that is, those who have through willfulness and stubbornness painted themselves into an impossible position. I was twelve years old and in trouble.

I could not retreat and keep my self-respect; this man of authority had made a fool of me in front of others and had, to me quite unjustifiably, subjected me to ridicule. I was resentful and hopelessly frustrated. I could not see a way out of my dilemma, and I was deeply distressed.

After a long time—no doubt it seemed much longer than it actually was, but it was a long time—I heard footsteps coming up our pathway from the front street, heard the pause and a murmured conversation at our back door, and then felt and heard him resume his pace toward me. Mother had told him where I was.

He came down the little passageway between our house and the coal shed, around the corner, and sat down beside me on the dirt. He said nothing for a time, but joined me as I nervously flipped little rocks and clods of dirt with a stick between my feet. I didn't look at him. After a time he spoke.

"Do you ever get up on Kotter's garage?" "Does Brother Kotter care?" "Do walnuts from the Perkinses' tree fall in your backyard?" "If you take ten shots at this hoop from the line over there, how many can you make?"

I gave brief answers to all questions, and again there was silence.

Then a large, strong hand reached over to my knee and grasped it warmly.

"Son," he said, "I made a mistake and I'm sorry."

"That's all right, Bishop," I said.

"Are you ready to go now?" he said. "The others are waiting."

"Okay," I said.

"We'd better get your pack ready."

He helped me roll the gear into the sleeping bag, secure it to the pack frame, and lift it to my back. We then walked out past our back door to the street and onto the truck where the others were waiting. I later learned that after I had left he called all of them together and explained that he had made a mistake and had been unkind to me and that my reaction had been understandable. He apologized to them in my behalf, prepared them to receive me without clamor when I arrived, got them all ready in the truck, and then made the long walk back to find me.

I do not dramatize what might have happened if a good man who was also a great man and a generous man had not made that long walk, if he had not been mature enough and humble enough and capable of acknowledging and correcting a mistake. I know I was wounded and frustrated by the impossibility of my circumstance. I know that he was the bishop we prayed for by name at our house every day. And I know that my wonderful mother, who did not intrude on my dilemma, must have helped pray him up the path.

I also know that boys and girls, even stubborn and rebellious ones, or hurt ones or bewildered ones, are worth something to our Heavenly Father and should be worth something to all the rest of His children. I do know that I myself have taken a few long walks when my own sense of pride or impatience might have prevailed, whispering to me: "Ah, let him go. Let him sit there and see how he likes it. Why should I be bothered?"

To this hour I remain grateful that my wonderful bishop overcame any such thoughts, if he had them, and made that long walk.

His light in my life has made a difference.

The Parable of the Unwise Bee

James E. Talmage

Sometimes I find myself under obligations of work requiring quiet and seclusion such as neither my comfortable office nor the cozy study at home insures. My favorite retreat is an upper room in the tower of a large building, well removed from the noise and confusion of the city streets. The room is somewhat difficult of access, and relatively secure against human intrusion. Therein I have spent many peaceful and busy hours with books and pen.

I am not always without visitors, however, especially in summertime; for, when I sit with windows open, flying insects occasionally find entrance and share the place with me. These self-invited guests are not unwelcome. Many a time I have laid down the pen, and, forgetful of my theme, have watched with interest the activities of these winged visitants, with an afterthought that the time so spent had not been wasted, for, is it not true, that even a butterfly, a beetle, or a bee, may be a bearer of lessons to the receptive student?

A wild bee from the neighboring hills once flew into the room; and at intervals during an hour or more I caught the pleasing hum of its flight. The little creature realized that it was a prisoner, yet all its efforts to find the exit through the partly opened casement failed. When ready to close up the room and leave, I threw the window wide, and tried at first to guide and then to drive the bee to liberty and safety, knowing well that if left in the room it would die as other insects there entrapped had perished in the dry atmosphere of the enclosure. The more I tried to drive it out, the more determinedly did it oppose and resist my efforts. Its erstwhile peaceful hum developed into an angry roar; its darting flight became hostile and threatening.

Then it caught me off my guard and stung my hand—the hand that would have guided it to freedom. At last it alighted on a pendant attached to the ceiling, beyond my reach of help or injury. The sharp pain of its unkind sting aroused in me rather pity than anger. I knew the inevitable penalty of its mistaken opposition and defiance; and I had to leave the creature to its fate. Three days later I returned to the room and found the dried, lifeless body of the bee on the writing table. It had paid for its stubbornness with its life.

To the bee's short-sightedness and selfish misunderstanding I was a foe, a persistent persecutor, a mortal enemy bent on its destruction; while in truth I was its friend, offering it ransom of the life it had put in forfeit through its own error, striving to redeem it, in spite of itself, from the prison-house of death and restore it to the outer air of liberty.

Are we so much wiser than the bee that no analogy lies between its unwise course and our lives? We are prone to contend, sometimes with vehemence and anger, against the adversity which after all may be the manifestation of superior wisdom and loving care, directed against our temporary comfort for our permanent blessing. In the tribulations and sufferings of mortality there is a divine ministry which only the godless soul can wholly fail to discern. To many the loss of wealth has been a boon, a providential means of leading or driving them from the confines of selfish indulgence to the sunshine and the open, where boundless opportunity waits on effort. Disappointment, sorrow, and affliction may be the expression of an all-wise Father's kindness.

Consider the lesson of the unwise bee!

"Trust in the Lord with all thine heart; and lean not unto thine own understanding. In all thy ways acknowledge him, and he shall direct thy paths." (Proverbs 3:5, 6).

$\mathscr{P}$utting the Kingdom of God First

REX PAUL GREENWOOD

During the winter of 1971, my companion and I were assigned to a "walking area" in Regina, Saskatchewan, Canada. The weather was not only cold and hostile, 20°–30° below zero, but so were some of the people.

After one particularly discouraging and bitterly cold day of knocking on door after door without having any success in finding someone who would invite us in out of the cold to give them our message of the restored gospel, we knocked on the door of a young lady that rather impressed us. She definitely wasn't too impressed with us, though, for she immediately informed us that we had interrupted her television program and slammed the door in our faces, after saying a few unkind words to us. In spite of her reception that matched the chilly Canadian weather, we still felt impressed that she was a choice and special spirit.

Three days later we were both surprised and delighted to find this young lady in church. One of the ward members had invited her to attend Sunday School with him and brought her into the investigators' class. The lesson, which was really the first discussion in the missionary lessons, interested her enough that she agreed to give us an appointment to give her the rest of the discussions.

We met with her twice a week to teach her the gospel and were amazed at how receptive she was to the gospel. Her understanding and appreciation of the gospel principles was exceptional. In fact, we found that she was also teaching her children the gospel in between our lessons, to help prepare them so that they could be baptized when she was.

Several weeks prior to the date set for the McLean family's

baptism, my companion and I had been in one of the local drugstores and had entered a contest for a Christmas turkey. Two days before the baptism we found out that we had actually won the turkey. We were eagerly looking forward to eating this turkey in a traditional American Christmas dinner, but the more we thought about it, the more we began to feel that a better approach would be to give the turkey to the McLean family on the day of their baptism. The mother was supporting herself and the four children, and her small salary did not allow for luxuries, sometimes not even for necessities, so we knew it would be appreciated.

The night after the baptismal service, which was Christmas Eve, we decided to take the turkey to the McLean home. We decided too that just a turkey wouldn't make much of a holiday dinner, so we went to the nearest supermarket, got a shopping cart and proceeded to fill it with all the trimmings needed to go with that turkey. No Christmas dinner would be complete without candied sweet potatoes, so we filled a small bag with sweet potatoes, and then filled as large a bag as we could find with white potatoes. We had a most delightful time filling other bags with vegetables, fruits, and canned goods. Of course, there had to be a generous bag of candy for the children. We couldn't have enjoyed ourselves more if we had been playing Santa Claus, until we got the groceries into the car and realized that we had just spent all of our food money for the week! There wasn't a supply of food in the cupboard back in our apartment, and we would not be receiving any money from home for another week. Nevertheless, we decided we would go ahead and give the food to the McLean family as we had planned, and hope for the best.

We stacked all the food into a huge cardboard box, put it on their doorstep, rang the bell, and ran. Never in my life have I seen anyone so happy as that family was when they looked out the window and saw that huge box of food. We were delighted to have been responsible for bringing happiness and joy to this sweet family at Christmastime, but we were also beginning to be quite concerned as to what was going to happen to us.

The next morning was a Sunday, so we went to church fasting—not because it was Fast Sunday, because it wasn't. We fasted out of necessity. After the meeting one of the members invited us to come to her home for Sunday dinner, and we gratefully accepted. That day, six more families requested that we join them for dinner that week, so we had a place to eat every day that week. We hadn't had even *one* person ask us to dinner in all the time we had been in Regina, and we had *seven* invitations that week!

We were quite impressed with the way the Lord had taken care of us as missionaries, but we were even more impressed when we learned that the McLean family had decided after their baptism that their first obligation as new members of the Church would be to pay their tithing. However, a quick check of their finances made it very clear that if they paid a full tithing it would require all of their funds and there would not be any money left to purchase the makings for a Christmas dinner. Since the McLeans were totally committed to the Church and its teachings, they decided to pay their tithing and leave Christmas dinner up to the Lord. Thus, right after the baptismal service, the McLeans paid their tithing for the first time.

Sister McLean testifies that our delivering the food for a Christmas dinner to their door was truly an answer to their prayers and a testimony to them that they will always be blessed *if* they will put the kingdom of God first and keep the commandments.

True Nobility

☆ EDGAR A. GUEST

Who does his task from day to day
And meets whatever comes his way,
Believing God has willed it so,
Has found real greatness here below.

Who guards his post, no matter where,
Believing God must need him there,
Although but lowly toil it be,
Has risen to nobility.

For great and low there's but one test:
'Tis that each man shall do his best.
Who works with all the strength he can
Shall never die in debt to man.

High Standards Attract

Boyd K. Packer

Several years ago I presided over one of our missions. Two of our missionaries were teaching a fine family who had expressed a desire to be baptized; and then they suddenly cooled off. The father had learned about tithing and he canceled all further meetings with the missionaries.

Two sad elders reported to the branch president, who himself was a recent convert, that he would not have this fine family in his branch.

A few days later the branch president persuaded the elders to join him in another visit to the family. "I understand," he told the father, "that you have decided not to join the Church."

"That is correct," the father answered.

"The elders tell me that you are disturbed about tithing."

"Yes," said the father. "They had not told us about it; and when I learned of it, I said, 'Now, that's too much to ask.' Our church has never asked anything like that. We think that's just too much and we will not join."

"Did they tell you about fast offering?" the president asked.

"No," said the man. "What is that?"

"In the Church we fast for two meals each month and give the value of the meals for the help of the poor."

"They did not tell us that," the man said.

"Did they mention the building fund?"

"No, what is that?"

"In the Church we all contribute toward building chapels. If you joined the Church, you would want to participate both in labor and with money. Incidentally, we are building a new chapel here," he told him.

"Strange," he said, "that they didn't mention it."

"Did they explain the welfare program to you?"

"No," said the father. "What is that?"

"Well, we believe in helping one another. If someone is in need or ill or out of work or in trouble, we are organized to assist, and you would be expected to help.

"Did they also tell you that we have no professional clergy? All of us contribute our time, our talents, our means, and travel—all to help the work. And we're not paid for it in money."

"They didn't tell us any of that," said the father.

"Well," said the branch president, "if you are turned away by a little thing like tithing, it is obvious you're not ready for this Church. Perhaps you have made the right decision and you should not join."

As they departed, almost as an afterthought he turned and said: "Have you ever wondered why people will do all of these things willingly? I have never received a bill for tithing. No one has ever called to collect it. But we pay it—and all of the rest— and count it as a great privilege.

"If you could discover *why,* you would be within reach of the pearl of great price, for which the Lord said the merchant man was willing to sell all that he had so that he might obtain it.

"But," the branch president added, "it is *your* decision. I only hope you will pray about it."

A few days later the man appeared at the branch president's home. No, he did not want to reschedule the missionaries. That would not be necessary. He wanted to schedule the baptism of his family. They had been praying, fervently praying.

This happens every day with individuals and entire families attracted by the high standards, not repelled by them.

The Workings
of the
Spirit

The Cross-Country Flight

Kris Mackay

Mr. Palmer? Mr. Dennis Palmer?"

"I'm Dennis Palmer."

Dennis looked up into the smiling eyes of a stewardess as she moved toward him down the aisle, holding in her hand what appeared to be some kind of passenger manifest. He flies often, and this was one more important cross-country business trip.

He was a little puzzled. Funny. He'd never before been asked to identify himself *after* boarding a flight. Must be something new.

The plane still sat on the ground at the Long Beach airport, but Dennis had already removed papers from a briefcase for his presentation in Chicago that afternoon and they were spread out across his lap. He planned to occupy himself during the flight with last-minute study.

The attractive young woman smiled again. Undoubtedly stewardesses are chosen partly for their ability to put passengers at ease.

"Do you live in California, Mr. Palmer? Were you born here?"

"I live in Orange County, but originally I came from Idaho."

"Have you ever been back East, say—to New York?"

"Yes, I have, as a matter of fact. I spent two years on the East Coast on a mission for my church, but that was a long time ago. Twelve years ago, at least."

The young woman rested her elbow against the seat in front of him, and leaned forward. "How interesting! Are you LDS?"

Just then the pilot started the plane's engines, and the stewardess stepped backwards, explaining hurriedly that she had preflight duties to complete. "After I'm finished I'll come back and talk to you again, if you don't mind."

Dennis watched her walk gracefully up the aisle, pausing to check a loose seat belt on the left or to give a final word of instruction to a novice traveler on the right. Then he pulled his attention back to the papers waiting on his lap.

Suddenly he realized he wasn't thinking of the facts and figures typed neatly on those pages. Though his eyes were dutifully scanning each line, his mind was elsewhere. Mention of his mission had sent his thoughts winging across the miles well ahead of the plane. In memory he was back in New York, living in a well-to-do suburb of Rochester where he and his companion rented a room with kitchen privileges. The few months spent in that area still bothered him. The trouble was that in spite of earnest and dedicated efforts he was afraid he hadn't accomplished anything really worthwhile.

They weren't accepted by their neighbors. True, most were congenial and spoke in passing, but these people were self-sufficient, able to take care of themselves. They felt no need for religious instruction.

The Elders contacted houses in the immediate vicinity and then moved on to tracting two or three miles away from home.

Neighborhood children were the bright spot of their day. Returning home in the evenings they were greeted with squeals of delight and nearly always stopped a minute to throw a football, play a game, or just tease one of the boys or girls good-naturedly as they would a younger brother or sister. Both were from large families, and their interaction with children filled a void in their lives at that time.

Eating lunch one day, they smiled, listening to sounds of fun in an adjoining yard. But abruptly the shouts of playing changed to screams of agony. The Elders dropped their sandwiches and bolted out of the door.

They ran to the backyard of the house next door and absorbed the grisly scene in one terrible glance. One young friend—a girl about six years old—lay screaming hysterically on the grass. She'd been sliding on a long, plastic slide coated by a stream of water from the hose, while her brother cut the lawn. Somehow she had slid into the mower. One portion of her tiny foot—from arch to upper heel—had been completely severed.

The girl's mother stood frozen in horror. Frantic, screaming children ran around in circles or raced out of the yard, unable to cope with the shock that confronted their eyes.

Blood poured from the ghastly wound. The Elders scooped up a towel that lay on the lawn by the slide and tore it in halves. Kneeling quickly at her side, they applied a tourniquet to her leg. She wouldn't last long if blood continued to escape at the rate it was going. Her mother ran inside for clean towels as the Elders administered a hasty blessing to the girl. One of them carried a key chain containing a small vial of consecrated oil.

The mother returned with fresh towels and they wrapped the injured foot securely. This was 1969. Reattachment of severed limbs was a fairly new process at that time. They picked up her mangled heel, gathered the little girl up in their arms, and started at once to get help. Fortunately an emergency facility was located only blocks from the house.

Doctors worked on her immediately. Elder Palmer and his companion waited tensely outside in the hallway. Before long the mother stepped out of the treatment room and into the hall. Looking at them with haggard eyes, she begged, "Will you come in and pray for my daughter?"

It's unusual to administer a second blessing within minutes of the first, but both felt that doing so would in this case be proper procedure. The mother wasn't present during the first one, and since she had asked for their help, they felt strongly impressed to offer her some form of tangible spiritual consolation.

A doctor worked at her feet while they put their hands on her head and promised, by the authority they held to act in God's name, that she would recover, that she would regain full use of her foot and suffer no permanent side effects—that she would be able to live a full and normal life and would walk without a limp.

As they spoke they were aware that the doctor stopped working. They left the room and he followed. He caught up to them in the hall.

He scowled. "How dare you hold out that ridiculous hope? Don't you realize that girl's Achilles' tendon has been severed? The main tendon that connects to the calf of the leg and affects movement of her whole little foot? She will require months or years of surgery and therapy. Possibly she will walk again—someday—but I doubt it. If she does, most assuredly it *won't* be without a limp!"

The missionaries left the hospital with the doctor's angry words ringing in their ears. A trifle discouraged, perhaps, but not wholly. They were convinced they had acted under a direction that superseded the doctor's.

Soon after that incident they were pulled out of the area and that part of the mission was closed. No other Elders took their place. They went on to other cities and were shortly involved in more productive work.

Three months later Elder Palmer and his new companion attended the Hill Cumorah pageant. Someone called his name, and glancing around he saw the little girl from Rochester. A cast covered the full length of her leg, and attempting to hurry to speak to him before the pageant started, she came, of course, with a *decided* limp. He didn't see her parents. Thousands of spectators sat at the foot of the hill. The pageant began, and after it was over their paths didn't cross.

Elder Palmer's mission was over. Before he left for home he stopped at mission headquarters and filled out a referral card in the name of the injured girl's parents.

His life from then on followed a typical returned-missionary pattern. He returned to school at Brigham Young University, graduated, married, moved to Southern California, and embarked on his career in business. His life was going well. But sometimes—like today—he couldn't help wondering about that little girl. . .

He was pulled from his reverie by the touch of a hand on his shoulder. The stewardess had come back and was speaking.

"You don't remember me, do you?" she laughed.

He looked at her closely. "No, I'm sorry. I don't. Have we met someplace before?"

She was—you may have already guessed—the little girl the doctor doubted would ever use her foot normally—walking without a trace of a limp and working in an occupation noted for seeking physical perfection in its employees. Missionaries had visited her family in response to the referral card, and all of their lives had been altered. Her father was a member of the high council; her mother was active in the ward Relief Society presidency; and her brother was currently on a mission.

As for the girl herself, she remembered that Elder Palmer came from somewhere in the west, and she searched for him on every flight. She wanted him to know that in less than a month she would be married in the Washington Temple.

When the plane landed in Chicago, Dennis almost floated off. He hardly needed to use the stairs.

This had been a memorable flight.

Hearken to the Spirit

Bruce R. McConkie

One of my earliest childhood recollections is of riding a horse through an apple orchard. The horse was tame and well broken, and I felt at home in the saddle.

But one day something frightened my mount, and he bolted through the orchard. I was swept from the saddle by the overhanging limbs, and one leg slipped down through the stirrup. I desperately hung to an almost broken leather strap that a cowboy uses to tie a lariat to his saddle. My weight should have broken the strap, but somehow it held for the moment. Another lunge or two of the stampeding horse would have broken the strap or wrenched it from my hands and left me to be dragged to injury or death with my foot entangled in the stirrup.

Suddenly the horse stopped, and I became aware that someone was holding the bridle tightly and attempting to calm the quivering animal. Almost immediately I was snatched up into the arms of my father.

What had happened? What had brought my father to my rescue in the split second before I slipped beneath the hoofs of my panic-driven horse?

My father had been sitting in the house reading the newspaper when the Spirit whispered to him, "Run out into the orchard!"

Without a moment's hesitation, not waiting to learn why or for what reason, my father ran. Finding himself in the orchard without knowing why he was there, he saw the galloping horse and thought, *I must stop this horse.*

He did so and found me. And that is how I was saved from serious injury or possible death.

$\mathcal{F}$ind Her

ALLAN K. BURGESS AND MAX H. MOLGARD

One night, Bette had a dream about a little girl and was told to find her. She realized that this was not going to be easy, because she only saw the girl from the back. Bette recorded in her journal that she seemed to be about six or seven years old and had long, dark, wavy hair down to her waist. She also seemed to have something wrong with her leg, because she was standing like it was hurt or handicapped.

Bette lived with her husband and family in Florida at the time. They already had four little children—ages six months, two, four, and five years old. They finally decided to approach an adoption agency because they didn't know any other way to find the little girl. After several months, they were accepted as worthy candidates to adopt a child. But they couldn't find her.

They waited for two years in Florida searching through hundreds of little faces in books of children awaiting adoption. They didn't feel that she was among any of them. They were then asked to transfer to San Diego, California. They prayed about it and didn't feel that it was the place in which they belonged. When they also turned down Mesa, Arizona, and asked for a transfer to Utah, they were told that there was only a one percent chance they would be able to move there.

They continued to pray for a move to Utah. When Bette's husband received a call at work and was told they could transfer to Tooele, Utah, he accepted immediately. He just felt it was right for his family.

They quickly called the adoption agency, thinking that the adoption records could be transferred. They were told that they would have to start the process all over again when they got to Utah. Bette was afraid that some day she would have to face

Heavenly Father and tell him that she hadn't found the child he told her about. But she didn't really feel that he was giving her a lot of help. Later she came to realize just how wrong she was.

Shortly after arriving in Utah, Bette discovered that she was expecting; they decided that this would be the little girl that she had seen. September found them with a new son instead.

Then her life was filled with complications. A teenage nephew moved in with them, thus raising her family to six children. She was called to be the ward Young Women's president, and a few weeks later developed a painful arthritic condition. She thought to herself that Heavenly Father would understand if she didn't pursue finding the little girl for a little while. By then things would surely settle down a little.

A few weeks later, her Young Women's counselor called to say that a badly abused girl had been brought into the medical center she worked in. She had been beaten with a two-by-four until most of her body was a seeping purple bruise. The counselor felt that she and her husband should become foster parents to the little girl. She was going to call her husband that night who was out of town with his work.

The counselor called the following day a little confused and said that her husband had told her that with their other obligations they wouldn't be able to spend the necessary time with a child that would need so much help. She couldn't understand why she had felt so strongly about being a foster parent to the abused girl. Both Bette and her counselor thought it was a little strange. Two days after her counselor had called, the still, small voice quit whispering and started shouting at Bette. The message was, "That is the little girl you've been looking for!"

Bette called her friend for a description of the girl and was told that she had dark hair down to her waist and was about six or seven years old. Her friend said that she could not tell Bette more, because she had only seen the girl from the back.

The next day Bette called the local family services, who told her that the girl was in temporary custody and would be returned to her natural family within the month. Bette felt confused but somewhat relieved because of her other pressures.

Just one week later, family services called Bette back. They said that the girl's situation had changed and they needed someone to take her in a long-term placement situation. Because Bette worked part-time in the office next door to theirs and they had come to know her, they said they could skip the necessary paper work and waiting period.

Leslie was placed in their home two days later. Family services told them that this was definitely a temporary placement. They also stressed that adoption was very unlikely.

Two and one-half years later, Leslie was adopted by Bette and her husband. Two weeks after that she was sealed to her new family in the Salt Lake Temple. One of the most spiritually stirring moments that those parents have ever experienced happened that day following the sealing. Leslie, dressed in a beautiful white dress, went around the sealing room hugging each person that was there and expressing to each one of them how much she loved them.

Bette learned a great lesson from this experience. She thought Heavenly Father wasn't helping to find Leslie, but he had to get the family transferred to Tooele and have Bette called as the ward Young Women's president so she could call as her counselor the person who worked at the medical clinic. He then had to help Bette become friends with the family services people so they would accept her as a foster mother on the spot. Now when Bette wonders if her prayers are being answered, she remembers this experience and waits patiently for the answer to come.

$\mathscr{A}$ Visit in the Rain

Kris Mackay

What constitutes a miracle? Often it comes unheralded—without trumpets or fanfare. Ordinary events in the lives of ordinary people take a sudden, unexpected twist. Participants in the drama sometimes act or react in a manner completely foreign to their normal personalities and, as a result, lives are changed—or saved.

Dana Lee, twelve years old, is never pushy. She's a quiet, gentle girl who is eager to please. That's why her attitude that rainy afternoon puzzled her mother. Dana wanted to stop at the huge department store to say hello to her sister Kim.

Sharon and Dana had been shopping, even though the weather was cold and blustery and they would have preferred to be at home, curled up in easy chairs in front of a toasty fire. Now their necessary purchases were completed, and Sharon wanted nothing more than to head for home as quickly as possible.

It was almost dinner time and they were both cold and tired. Ordinarily Dana would go along with her mother's wishes, but apparently not today. She insisted. Why did she have to see Kim *today?* She couldn't offer a plausible explanation; she just stubbornly stuck to her resolve, which was so surprising in itself that Sharon went against her own inclinations and gave in.

Kim was the oldest of the three Lee girls, the only one married, and was six months pregnant with Sharon and Mike's first grandchild. This was an exciting time. Kim clerked at a major department store, but Sharon and Dana didn't even know which area of the store she would be in on that particular day. She was a temporary "flyer," sent to any section that ran short-handed on any given afternoon.

Stopping to say hello would entail first going upstairs to the main office to check the flyer board. Sloshing through the downpour wasn't worth the effort. Kim would be through work in a couple of hours and they could telephone her at her apartment. Sharon looked at Dana hopefully. Wouldn't that be okay? No! Dana wanted to see her now!

Sharon shook her head in disbelief at her daughter's insistence, and turned the key in the ignition. Peering through the windshield between swipes of the wiper, she drove the car in the direction of the store's parking lot.

After parking the car and dashing to the store's entrance, they shook the rain from their coats and headed for the escalator. But for some reason, Sharon paused as they passed the elevator and found herself pushing the button. She'd never taken the elevator before. Always she'd automatically stepped onto the moving staircase. Her only rationale, in thinking back to that day, may have been that the elevator is faster, considerably faster than the escalator, and she was in a hurry to head for home. In any case, they took the elevator and then checked the flyer board to pinpoint where they could find Kim.

This time—also without conscious decision—they headed toward the *escalator* to return to the main floor. Why didn't they take the elevator? Sharon has no logical answer. The elevator was still faster, of course (that hadn't changed), and she was still in a hurry to get home. All she can say is that that was not the route they found themselves taking.

They neared the escalator and were pleasantly surprised to see Kim walking toward them. She hadn't spotted them yet. Plagued from time to time with uncomfortable bouts of nausea, today was one of the worst. She'd asked to be excused from her work station long enough to get a snack from the cookie bar on the second floor. She carried a small bag of cookies in one hand and a carton of milk in the other.

Sharon watched her daughter's approach. Like mothers everywhere, it hurt her to see the look of pale weakness on her daughter's pretty face. Fortunately the months were passing swiftly and this stage of the pregnancy should be over and done with very soon. Sharon smiled. Feeling ill was hard, but it would pass. None of them doubted that the baby was worth the effort. Certainly not Kim. Having this new precious life to love and lavish her attention on was all that mattered in the end.

Sharon, Dana, and Kim met at the top of the escalator. If prior arrangements had been made, their meeting could not have been more exact. Kim and Dana, talking excitedly, synchronized their movements and balanced on the top stair, moving forward and starting smoothly down, while Sharon settled onto the step behind them.

Suddenly, without warning of any kind, the escalator ground to an abrupt, lurching stop. Its arrested momentum pitched the two girls forward. Falling head first, Dana frantically grabbed for the railing. Kim's hands were filled, and in the fraction of a second it would take to open her fingers and drop her milk and cookies, the chance to help herself would be gone. Like life passing instantly before a dying person's eyes, she pictured her body somersaulting from step to step until she came to rest in a heap at the bottom. What would that do to her unborn child?

But she had not taken into account the quick reaction of her mother. Perhaps nobody else would have been able to move as quickly; certainly nobody else would have had as much to lose. Somehow Sharon managed to maintain her balance as both hands shot out to rescue her children—and her grandchild.

With Dana clutching for the rail and Kim bent nearly double, falling out of control with her head frighteningly near to crashing against the next step, Sharon seized a handful of each girl's clothing, dug her heels in, and hung on fiercely. The force of their forward propulsion was so severe that even her stopping them was a jolt, but, of course, a jolt highly preferable to the alternative.

After regaining their footing, they helped each other walk safely, if shakily, down the stairs. The baby's life had been spared.

Why did Dana insist on stopping to say hello to her sister on a day when it was anything but convenient?

Why did they ride the elevator, which allowed them to reach the top of the escalator the very second Kim stepped on and began her descent?

Why did all these apparently unrelated actions take place on the only day the escalator has ever failed in the history of the store?

I wonder. But along with the Lees and the Haycocks, I'm pretty sure I know.

*L*eave for West Berlin Today

DIETER BERNDT

In 1960, I was living near Hamburg in West Germany and was called to be the mission YMMIA president. Half of the members of our mission lived in East Germany, which necessitated having counterpart Young Men's and Young Ladies' presidents serving in the same capacity in East Germany. Because the Church members were scattered over a large area, we made a special effort to plan as many activities as possible that could be attended by all the youth of the mission. This presented some problems peculiar to our mission, since half the mission was in West Germany and West Berlin, and the other half was behind the iron curtain. It was impossible to hold any activities in the eastern sector, so we scheduled all of our programs in West Berlin so that East Germans could also attend. They could easily board a subway in East Berlin, ride across the border into West Berlin and attend the meeting, then return to their homes without difficulty.

Shortly after I was called to this position, we began planning for our most important and largest activity of the year, which was to be a youth conference to be held in West Berlin during the Easter holiday. I began corresponding with the Young Men's and Young Women's presidents in East Germany and managed to complete all the arrangements for the conference by mail.

The conference was a tremendous success—very inspiring and very enjoyable. For me, the most interesting part on the program was a musical number by a very attractive and talented young lady—the Young Women's president from East Germany with whom I had been corresponding.

I immediately took advantage of the first opportunity to become acquainted with Gisaliela and was even more impressed with her as I got to know her. During the months that followed, our correspondence continued, and before long we began meeting in West Berlin whenever possible. We began to make plans for our future together and made the necessary unauthorized arrangements for her to come to Hamburg to meet my family during her vacation. Gisaliela's mother was to accompany her to East Berlin on Tuesday, August 15, where they would spend the night with her brother before continuing on to West Berlin to pick up their airline tickets for Hamburg.

The Sunday morning before Gisaliela was due to arrive, Mother and I attended church services in Hamburg as usual, but the priesthood meeting did not proceed as usual—it was announced that the Berlin Wall had been put up during the night and *all* traffic between East and West Berlin had been terminated! I was heartsick. The girl I wanted to marry was in East Germany and she would not be permitted to leave. This meant that we could not be married as we had planned.

I was so upset by this news that I decided that I would leave immediately for West Berlin to see if there was something that I could do to make arrangements for Gisaliela to leave East Germany. Knowing full well the futility of trying to deal with the Communist-controlled government, Mother told me that there was no point in my going to Berlin, for she was sure that there was nothing I could do.

I was very discouraged and dejected that Sunday morning as Mother and I knelt in prayer and asked the Lord for his help. We hoped, and prayed fervently, that somehow the Lord would help us so that Gisaliela and I could be reunited.

I was so disheartened that I couldn't concentrate on what any of the speakers had to say or on the lessons. I returned home and found that a telegram from Gisaliela was waiting for me. I couldn't believe it—she was in *West* Berlin! It was unbelievable, incomprehensible! She was not due in West Berlin for several more days!

The following Friday Gisaliela arrived at the Hamburg airport. She then told me the following story of how she came to be in West Berlin on that Saturday afternoon a few hours before the Berlin Wall went up:

"Saturday morning I was busy preparing for a district meeting when my father came into the room and said, 'I want you to leave for West Berlin today.' I replied that Mother and I had made all the arrangements to leave on Tuesday, and besides, I had to prepare for the district meeting, but my father insisted that we leave for West Berlin immediately! When I asked for a reason why we should leave early, his only reply was that he didn't know why—he just *knew* that we should leave as soon as possible.

"I couldn't understand this—it was so unlike my father to irrationally and illogically make this type of decision. I asked him again for a good reason and he said, 'I can't give you a good reason. I just have this uneasy feeling and I feel impressed that you should leave now for West Berlin.' He refused to discuss the matter further and told my mother that she was to leave with me and cautioned us not to make any stops along the way.

"He was so determined that Mother and I decided to do as he asked. We packed our bags and were on the next train to Berlin. We found out later that this was the last train we could have taken to Berlin. There were no more tickets sold after that train departed.

"We had previously planned to spend our first evening in East Berlin with my brother and in a day or two cross over into West Berlin and pick up our airline tickets at a friend's home. For some reason, we decided to continue on to the friend's house to pick up the tickets, with the intention of returning to East Berlin that evening and spending the night. However, when we picked up the tickets our friend suggested that we spend the night, so, quite contrary to our plans, we accepted the invitation and spent the night in West Berlin.

"You can imagine the shock we experienced when we awoke the next morning and found that the Berlin Wall had gone up during the night and the border had been closed. Even now, it's hard to comprehend that such a thing could actually happen. I'm so very grateful that my Heavenly Father inspired my earthly father to have me leave the day before the wall was constructed. I'm also thankful that I was obedient and listened to his inspired advice.

"Mother, of course, wanted to be with my father, who was the branch president, so she returned to East Germany that morning. We parted with heavy hearts, not knowing when, or if ever we would see each other again."

When Gisaliela related her experience to me, I knew that the Lord had opened the way for us to be married and that our marriage would be very special, and it has been.

The Lord has truly blessed us and allowed us to be brought together by forces that cannot be explained by human powers. The power of the Holy Ghost to guide and inspire each of us is real. Gisaliela and I can bear witness that this is so, for our lives have been altered dramatically by obeying the promptings of the still small voice. A miracle was truly performed in our behalf.

Jesus, Listening, Can Hear

Jean Ernstrom

It has been two weeks and I am still deeply touched how in one fleeting moment, with great power, the Spirit was manifest to me through two bright blue eyes. The eyes belong to Heather, a nine-year-old-girl with a keen mind, infectious giggle, and a determined spirit housed in a very physically restricted frame. Due to the nature of her handicaps, the simplest of life's activities, if at all possible, are a major task. Unable to verbalize, Heather sends messages, quite efficiently, with her eyes; a direct gaze indicating "yes" and a blink meaning "no." So through a series of questions, gazes, blinks, giggles, facial expressions, more questions and more gazes and blinks, Heather has shared her vibrant spirit and brought incredible amounts of joy into the lives of those who know her and take the time to interact with her.

As Heather's therapist and teacher for the past four years, I have sensed on many occasions that for Heather, as with other handicapped children, the veil seems to be very thin. How often I have wondered what *she* could teach *me* about the things of the Spirit if only the expression were granted.

Heather is proud of her membership in The Church of Jesus Christ of Latter-day Saints and is a great little missionary in her own right as she struggles to share with others that which is of most value to her.

Summer school is a fun time for special students and teachers alike. The atmosphere is relaxed and the days are short. Its purpose is to maintain basic living skills during the long break between school years.

Monday morning, as usual, Heather arrived at school with a countenance as bright as the sun in the sky. As she was wheeled off the bus, we visited about the previous weekend. When we arrived at the classroom, Heather indicated to me that she had attended Primary so I began singing some of the Primary songs, looking for an indication of familiarity on Heather's face. A smile broke across her face in immediate recognition. Between songs I talked to Heather briefly and she responded in her usual manner. I asked Heather if I could sing my favorite Primary song "I Wonder When He Comes Again." She responded positively and so I proceeded. At the conclusion of that song I asked Heather if she had a favorite song. Immediately her eyes focused on mine but then I faced the challenge of determining which song she loved above all others and to satisfy my own curiosity—why? Through a series of questions I discovered that it was a song she had heard in Primary. She wasn't sure which songbook it was in and most importantly, it was a song about Jesus. . . . I went through every possible song I could think of. To my dismay and Heather's disappointment, none of them were the right one. I didn't understand and concluded that Heather was confused. I had spent eight years collectively as Junior Primary Chorister and felt certain that I had not forgotten any of the songs about Jesus. But Heather refused to let the issue die. It was as if she needed for some reason for the two of us to share her favorite song. Finally I agreed that I would bring my Primary song books to school the following day and promised her that we would go through them together.

Tuesday morning Heather arrived and was wheeled into the classroom. Visually she was on the prowl for the songbooks. As her eyes fixed on the books across the room, she gave me a squeal and a look to let me know in no uncertain terms that she wanted to find the song—now! So we took a minute and went through the books, but to no avail. She liked all of the songs but none of them were *the* song.

Wednesday dawned a beautiful day. It was as if the day were created to reflect the beauty of what lay in store. Heather came to school more determined than ever that we find her song. Tucked in Heather's wheelchair was the new hymnbook. I took Heather out of her wheelchair and situated her comfortably on her stomach in a beanbag. I positioned myself on the floor at her side. Page by page we made our way through the hymnbook. With each page I sang the first phrase of the song and with each page Heather's eyes closed in a definite no. We were more than halfway through the book and I'm afraid I began to doubt the possibility of any success in the adventure but I continued. As a matter of routine I turned to the next page and began: "There is sunshine in my soul today . . ."

It was as if someone had stuck her with a pin. Heather jumped and smiled; her bright eyes looking directly my way. Together we laughed and reveled in the moment of completing a three day search. With the search ended it was time to get back to business. . . . Once she was situated in her chair with her head resting comfortably on my arm I said, "OK, now we can finally sing your favorite song." With a smile on her face she listened as I began:

> "There is sunshine in my soul today,
> More glorious and bright
> Than glows in any earthly sky,
> For Jesus is my light."

As I began the chorus Heather mustered all the effort she could and joined in with occasional sounds only slightly more audible than a sigh but booming with spirit to sing with me . . .

> "Oh, there's sunshine, blessed sunshine
> When the peaceful happy moments roll.
> When Jesus shows his smiling face,
> There is sunshine in the soul."

As I sang the words to the last line she looked at me steadily, as if to say, "I like that part." I felt so grateful that we had found the song. Heather was so happy that it was worth the effort and then some. Little did I realize that the real message was yet to be discovered. I asked if she wanted the rest of the verses. She, of course, responded with a firm, "Yes." . . . So I continued:

"There is music in my soul today,
A carol to my King,
And Jesus listening can hear
The songs I cannot sing . . ."

And Jesus, listening, can hear the songs I cannot sing. Heather seemed to really come to life at that line in the song. Her reaction was so strong that I stopped. I looked at her as the reality and significance of the moment pressed on my mind. I queried, "Heather, is that it? Is that what you like about the song? Is it what you want me to know? That Jesus is listening and He can hear the songs *you* cannot sing?" She lifted her head and looked me straight in the eyes with excitement and yet almost relief evident on her face. The testimony had been borne.

I felt a great reverence at what was taking place. Feeling guided by the Spirit myself I ventured on to ask, "Heather, does Jesus talk to you in your mind and in your heart?" Immediately her little head again came up and her look was penetrating.

Knowing her close relationship with the Savior and feeling surely an answer awaited, there was one more thing I wanted to know. So with reverent anticipation I whispered, "Heather, what does He say?" My heart pounded as I viewed the clear look in her eyes as she awaited my questions so she could in fact share with me her insight. I feel that the Lord gave me the right questions to ask as I took a deep breath and proceeded. "Does He say, 'Heather, I *love* you'?" Her eyes were simply radiant as she confirmed that statement. I paused, swallowed and continued, "Does He say, 'Heather, you're *special*'?" With a newfound energy source her arms began to wave with excitement and her eyes were as big as quarters as she looked into my face. I paused again with a lump in my throat and then followed with, "Does He say, 'Heather, be patient, I have *great* things in store for you'?"

What I next witnessed, I will never forget. Heather's head became erect; every fiber of her being seemed to be electrified as her eyes penetrated my own soul. She *knew* she was loved.

She *knew* she was special. She *knew* she needed only be patient, for great things are in store.

The moment was too sacred for further words. I leaned forward and pressed her cheek against my own. Without any words, but with bright blue eyes as windows to a valiant soul, the truth was made known.

Yes, Heather, Jesus, listening, *can* hear.

*T*hat Is the Worst Lesson I've Ever Heard!

ALLAN K. BURGESS AND MAX H. MOLGARD

The new missionary district leader could not believe what he was hearing. He was listening to Elder Parker, who had been out for almost two years, stumble his way through the first discussion. Any missionary of worth who had been out three weeks or longer knew the first discussion, but Elder Parker didn't. The early morning study session came to a close and Elder Parker left with his companion.

The new district leader turned to his companion, shook his head and said, "That's the worst first discussion I have ever heard. Isn't Elder Parker dedicated enough to learn the discussions?" His companion was surprised that he did not know the discussion; he had always felt that Elder Parker was an excellent missionary.

The next day was their first district meeting of the month, and each of the companionships was to come prepared to share its goals for the new month. It was not an easy mission to baptize in, and the baptism goal of each companionship ranged from three to five people. Then it was Elder Parker's turn to share his baptism goal for the month. When he said that they were planning on baptizing twenty people that month, the district leader almost laughed out loud. He thought to himself, *Elder Parker doesn't even know the first discussion but is going to baptize twenty people. This I have to see.*

The next week when the missionaries met, the only Elders who had baptized were Elder Parker and his companion. They had baptized five people. The district leader wanted to see how Elder Parker could baptize so many despite his not knowing the discussions, so he asked to go with Elder Parker the next time he was going to teach a first discussion.

The next day, the district leader received a phone call and was invited to go with Elder Parker the following morning to help him teach the first discussion to an interested family. In those days, the discussions were memorized and given almost word for word. Missionaries would take turns, each giving a few paragraphs and shifting back and forth so it seemed like an informal discussion. Elder Parker started the discussion and completely murdered the first part. The district leader took his turn and tried to bring some order back to the flow of the discussion. It was then Elder Parker's turn again—he completely skipped several key paragraphs. By the end of the lesson, the district leader was totally disoriented and confused. He felt that the family probably felt the same way.

When the discussion was over, Elder Parker leaned forward and put his hand on the arm of the family's father. He then looked him straight in the eyes, told him how much he loved him and his family, and bore one of the most humble and powerful testimonies that the district leader had ever heard. By the time he finished, every member of the family, including the father, and both Elders had tears running down their cheeks. Next Elder Parker taught the father how to pray, and they all knelt down while the father prayed that they might receive testimonies of their own and thanked Heavenly Father for the great love that he felt. Two weeks later the whole family was baptized.

As they were driving away from the discussion, Elder Parker apologized to the district leader. He told him that he felt very bad that he did not know the discussions better. He said that he had always had a problem with memorization. He said that he got up at five-thirty instead of six o'clock every morning and spent two hours on the discussions but could never remember them well when it came time to teach them. He explained that he knelt in prayer before teaching each family and talked with Heavenly Father about his problem. He would ask Heavenly Father to bless him so that when he bore his testimony the people would feel his love and the Spirit and know that they were being taught the truth.

Humbled, the district leader spent the rest of the day pondering what he had learned about teaching the gospel. For the first time he realized that it was not discussions but love and the Spirit that converted people to the gospel. The district leader never taught the gospel the same way again.

"We've Been Waiting for You"

GRANT H. TAYLOR

While serving as a Latter-day Saint missionary in Denmark, I found myself in a great complex of apartment buildings on the outskirts of Copenhagen. I had recently received a new companion with whom I was not particularly thrilled. He later turned out to be one of my favorite companions, but at the moment he was slow and dumb and generally useless. I was cross because we had tracted all afternoon and had met nothing but mean, discourteous, abusive, and even foul-smelling people. It was a pretty glum day.

We looked through our tracting book to check on the possibility of any callbacks in the area. I hoped we wouldn't find any, because it was pretty close to dinnertime. In my state of frustration I felt that I wouldn't be much of a messenger for the Lord anyway. But to my disappointment we found listed in the book two callbacks in the next building. So we checked them out. The first one wasn't at home (or, I should say, no one answered the door), and the second one said he had thought about it and had decided he wasn't interested.

When we turned to leave, my graceful companion stumbled and fell against the wall, hitting the doorbell of the adjacent apartment. Silently praising his unique talents, I accepted the fact that we would just have to stand there and pretend that we had forgotten that we had called at this door just last week. I vaguely remembered the door and the man who had answered it. I was preparing a sort of apology in my mind as the door opened, but this time it was a large, friendly-looking woman who appeared. I switched speeches and just gave her a regular door approach. She seemed to be staring intently at me all the time I was speaking. I thought at first that she must be deaf and was reading my lips, but I found out later that I was quite wrong.

I finished the approach, and then I heard something that I had heard other misisonaries mention but that I had always believed no one ever hears in actuality. The woman said, to our disbelieving ears, "Come in. We've been waiting for you."

We tried not to look too amazed as we went in and were greeted by the man we had seen the week before and by two young boys. The family turned out to be Herr and Fru Vestergaard and their sons, Kurt and Poul.

We returned regularly to the Vestergaard home and presented the series of lessons, which they accepted almost before even hearing them. Both boys were under eight years of age, so when it came time to issue the baptism challenge we made plans for just Brother and Sister Vestergaard. The baptismal service was the most beautiful of my entire mission, and that family is still very close to my heart. They were marvelous people, and I often wondered how we had been so blessed to find them on such an unpleasant day and to have such an easy time teaching them.

One evening following one of Sister Vestergaard's fabulous roast pork dinners, and just before my transfer from Copenhagen, Sister Vestergaard told me something that answered many questions. "You know," she said, "it was not without reason that you and your companion were admitted into our home that afternoon several weeks ago. And furthermore, I knew immediately when I saw you that you had brought the truth from God to my family."

I began reflecting on that day involving the doorbell incident, and could clearly remember how I had sensed that this woman was staring unnaturally at me, and how astonished we had been when we were welcomed into their home so warmly with those unbelievable words, "We've been waiting for you."

Sister Vestergaard then related this story to me: It seems that she and her husband had been sincerely looking for some spiritual direction for their family. They had attended many different churches and had been receiving missionaries and representatives from several of them regularly. They felt a need for religion in their home as their boys grew up, but they seemed unable to find satisfaction.

"During these months of investigation," Sister Vestergaard continued, "I kept having this strange dream in which I always saw a face." Nothing was ever spoken, and no significance ever seemed apparent, she said, but it occurred several times. Always the same face—never speaking and never indicating any significance. "Finally I began to feel somewhat concerned," she said.

Weeks passed with no change, and she and her husband had pretty well decided to settle on membership in one of the soliciting neighborhood churches. But then one afternoon, just as they were sitting down to the evening meal, the doorbell rang. It seemed like an unusually long ring. "I went to the door," Sister Vestergaard said, "and opened it to find two young men. I immediately recognized one of them. At first I couldn't recall from where. Then suddenly I knew, and at the same instant I knew that they had been sent to my home by the God I had been so sincerely seeking.

"You see, Elder Taylor," she said, "the face I had seen so many times in my dream was your face."

Physical Riches in Exchange for a Covenant Family

ALLAN K. BURGESS

Members of the Church living in Tonga prior to 1983 had a difficult time taking advantage of the covenants and blessings available in the temple. The closest temple to Tonga was in New Zealand, and most Tongan families could not afford to make the long and expensive journey.

One family in Tonga received strong spiritual promptings that they should travel to New Zealand and obtain their temple blessings. In order to do so, they would need to sell all that they owned, including their modest hut. They made the decision that obedience to the Holy Ghost and receiving the blessings of the temple were more important than any earthly possessions, so they proceeded to sell all of their furniture and personal belongings. They found that they could get more for their hut if they dismantled it and sold each piece separately, so this is what they did. Their friends in the Church made fun of them and tried to talk them out of their "foolishness." The family was told over and over again that God did not expect them to sacrifice everything they had in order to go to the temple. They responded that they could not speak for others, but they knew that this is what God wanted their family to do.

This devoted family traveled to New Zealand and eagerly partook of the spirit and blessings of the temple. Just two weeks after they returned home, a hurricane swept through their area and destroyed everything in its path. Everyone around them lost their homes and all of their belongings. The family quickly realized the temple trip had actually cost them nothing, for they would have lost everything anyway. Because they had been responsive to the whisperings of the Spirit, even though they possessed no physical riches, they enjoyed the precious promises and blessings of a covenant family.

Teaching
by
Example

Sept. 23, 2004

$\mathcal{M}$r. Brimhall

GEORGE D. DURRANT

Mr. Brimhall was my fifth-grade teacher at the old Harrington Elementary School in American Fork.

Mr. Brimhall acted as if he was so mean. I too thought he was mean back then. I recall that some said, "Mr. Brimhall is mean. But he's fair, because he's mean to *everybody*."

But, you know, I once said to myself, *he wasn't mean at all.* How could a mean teacher have been so kindly aware of an insecure little guy like me? How could a mean teacher have said to me almost every day, "George, it's a little noisy out in the hall. You are our official door-closer. Would you get up and go close the door?"

At this request I would go to the door, close it, and return to my seat. Mr. Brimhall would say, "Thank you, George. You are a good door-closer." I'd feel as though I were the most important person in the class and maybe even in the whole world, and that Mr. Brimhall was the world's kindest man.

I knew that being asked to close the door didn't have anything to do with arithmetic. I seldom could have been praised for my prowess in that area. But I knew Mr. Brimhall was right—I was a good door-closer. And somehow that made up for a lot of things I wasn't so good at.

One day we were studying fractions. Mr. Brimhall said, "If you had four quarters of a pie, they would all be equal in size." He added, "The four quarters of anything are all equal in size."

I raised my hand and, mustering all my courage, said, "Mr. Brimhall, that's not right."

"Oh?" he said in sort of a mean way. "When is it not right?"

I timidly replied, "Well, my dad shot a deer, and I was helping him cut it up. The hindquarters were a lot bigger than the front ones."

The twenty-nine other students all laughed at my remark. I suddenly found myself wishing I'd kept quiet as I usually did.

Mr. Brimhall didn't laugh. He stood up from his chair and walked over to where I sat. He stood above me, put his hand on my shoulder, and softly said, "I've never thought of it like that. You are absolutely right. George, you've got what I call common sense, and that is the best kind of sense."

I had lowered my head when all the other students had laughed at what I'd said. But when Mr. Brimhall said that, I looked up, and in a sense I saw the sky.

I'll always remember that moment when a kind teacher who knew something about the insecurity of a little boy caused me to look up. In a small way, from that moment on I was never quite the same.

*W*hat Religion Can Produce a Young Man like That?

MARION D. HANKS

Not long ago and not far away a boy entered a pharmacist's shop, told the proprietor that he was Bob Brown, son of Mrs. Helen Brown, and inquired whether there was any possibility for him to work at the pharmacy to pay for medicine that the store owner had supplied to the family but for which he had not yet been paid. Mr. Jones didn't really need any additional help, but he was so impressed by the unusual conscientiousness of this seventeen-year-old high school boy that he made arrangements for Bob to work at the store part-time on Saturdays.

That first day of diligent work greatly impressed the businessman, who at the completion of it handed the young man an envelope containing twelve dollars—the wages agreed upon. The boy took two one-dollar bills from the envelope and asked Mr. Jones to give him change for one of them. Bob put the other dollar bill and twenty cents in his pocket, deposited the eighty cents change in the envelope with the ten-dollar bill, and handed the money to Mr. Jones to apply to the family account, asking if that division of wages was agreeable to the pharmacist.

Mr. Jones tried to insist that Bob keep a larger portion of the money. "You'll need some money for school," he said, "and besides, I've already decided to increase your pay in the future. Why don't you keep at least half of the twelve dollars?"

"No, sir," said the seventeen-year-old. "Maybe later I could keep a little more, but today I would like to pay the ten dollars and eighty cents on our bill."

At that moment some of Bob's friends came by and invited him to attend a movie with them. He said he couldn't, that he had to go home. They continued to tease him to go with them until finally he informed them firmly that he didn't have any money and couldn't go with them. Mr. Jones, observing all of this, was about to intervene again to offer money to Bob when one of the boys who had playfully jostled him heard the twenty cents rattle in Bob's pocket. The bantering began again, because obviously he did have some money. Quietly Bob finally said: "Look, guys, I do have a little money but it isn't mine; it's my tithing. Now take off, will you, please. I need to get home to see how Mom's doing."

When Bob and the others had left the store, Mr. Jones went to the telephone and called a physician friend. "Doctor," he said, "I have been filling your prescriptions for years and have long admired your reputation as a fine surgeon. I've also known you are a Mormon bishop, but I have never had any interest in your religion. But I now have one of your boys working for me who is so different that I need to learn about a religion that can produce a young man like that."

Arrangements were made, and the pebble dropped into the life of Mr. Jones by Bob Brown began the extending circles that to this point have gently washed the druggist and members of his family and many others into a warm, loving life as fellow citizens with the Saints in the household of God.

Example Opened the Door

KEVIN STOKER

In January 1954, George and Truena Love were surprised to receive a phone call from two sister missionaries who said they were at the bus station in Ruston, Louisiana. The Loves, Ruston's only LDS family, invited Sister Leta E. Bartholomew and her companion to their home and helped them search for an apartment.

The sisters searched and searched, but with little more than one hundred dollars a month to live on the pair found most lodgings too expensive. Finally one lady referred them to the Tutens, an older couple who had rented in the past.

When Edgar L. Tuten, Jr., answered the door, the sisters introduced themselves as missionaries from The Church of Jesus Christ of Latter-day Saints. Edgar said that he thought what they were doing was commendable but that he wasn't interested in renting out the apartment. He then asked where the sisters were from. When they said Utah and Idaho, he exclaimed, "Utah! That's where the *Mormons* are."

The sisters said they were Mormon missionaries, and Edgar promptly invited them into his house. After some discussion, he asked if Ezra Taft Benson, then Secretary of Agriculture, was a member of their Church. They answered, "He is one of our Church's Twelve Apostles."

"Yes," Edgar said with a smile. "I know. He's a good man, and I like him. I admire him for what he's doing. He believes in something, and he's sticking to it. He has integrity and honesty. He's doing what he thinks is right."

After a brief pause, Edgar said he still didn't want to rent the apartment, but if the missionaries were interested they could stay in the apartment free. "Anyone who's a member of the same church as Ezra Taft Benson is welcome to these rooms, and we're proud to have you," he said.

"The apartment was one of the cleanest and nicest places in which I lived as a missionary," Sister Bartholomew remembers. "It was centrally located, and, best of all, it was owned by our landlords and friends, the Tutens."

Before the sisters left Ruston, they taught the Tutens the gospel and left them a Book of Mormon. "As we waved good-bye, each wiping a tear or two from our faces," Sister Bartholomew relates, "I remembered how this special friendship had begun, and how two missionary sisters had been blessed with a clean, comfortable, well-located apartment—because of the righteous influence of President Benson on a man he never met."

Caught Speeding

S. Dilworth Young

Many years ago I was driving home late one night from Provo to take care of my sick wife. I was very nervous because I had prepared things for her to last until six o'clock at night, and I was starting home from Provo at eleven o'clock at night, so she had already been without help for five hours. I was fit to be tied. I passed through Salt Lake City (I had not been arrested so far between there and Provo), and started up the highway toward Ogden, got as far as Farmington junction, and turned off on to the hill road, newly paved at that time though not straightened out. With that I stepped on that accelerator and got the car going seventy miles an hour. I passed the road where Hill Field takes off going seventy-two or -three; it was downhill a bit, and going down the hill I think I increased to seventy-eight or eighty. And then I noticed through my rear-view mirror the flashing light of the patrol car. I pulled to a stop and got out and walked back fifteen or twenty feet, extending my hands so he could see I was not armed, and he came up and stopped a few feet away and got out.

"I guess you're arresting me for speeding," I said.

"Yes, you were doing better than sixty miles an hour when you passed the Hill Field road."

"I was doing better than seventy miles an hour when I passed the Hill Field road," I corrected him. "But give me a ticket; I've got to go. My wife's sick, I'm in a hurry, and I'll pay the fine gladly, but let me get out of here. I've got to go home quickly, so just give me the ticket."

He said, "Don't get your shirt off. Stand still a minute. I'm not going to give you a ticket." He had not asked for my name. He just stood there.

I said, "Well, thanks for that."

He continued, "I'm going to give you a warning ticket. That means you don't have to go to court unless you do it again. On one condition."

"What's the condition?" I asked.

"That you drive within the speed limit the rest of the way home, so you will get to your wife."

I said, "I'll do it."

So he gave me the ticket and when he handed it to me it had my name on it. He smiled, stuck out his hand, and said, "My name's Bybee. I used to be one of your Scouts at Camp Kiesel."

All the way home I said to myself, with each turn of the wheels on my car, "What if I'd lied to him? He knew I was doing seventy. Policemen do. He knew I was going too fast, and he knew I was his Scout executive years before, too." I did not know that he knew any of this, but if I had not told him the exact truth or tried to hedge at all he would have lost respect. He would have given me a ticket, and I would have had no influence on that man ever again.

*J*immy

GEORGE D. DURRANT

Editor's Note: George D. Durrant began his career with the Church Educational System in Brigham City, Utah, where the Intermountain Indian School for young Navajo students was located. Part of his assignment was to teach seminary to these shy and promising youth. This story reflects the rewards of that experience.

I recall fifteen-year-old Jimmy. He was a troublemaker and wasn't shy by any standards. His boisterousness was downright disruptive not only to his own class but to our other seven classes. Jimmy would never listen to a lesson.

About midyear I decided that I as a teacher was saying too much and the students were saying too little in our lessons. The only answers they ever gave were "yes" or "no." I decided that I would change that. I'd get them to talk. So on a special day I said, "I brought some popcorn today. Let's all sit around and eat it, and as we eat we'll talk about what Heavenly Father is like."

I set the stage as well as I could and then softly said, "Now, you each tell me what you feel about our Heavenly Father." For a few minutes all was silent except for the crunching of popcorn.

I gently said, "Robert, do you believe in Heavenly Father?"

The only response I got was some crunching.

"Albert, what about you?"

More seconds of silence, except for crunching.

I gently asked, "Albert, do you believe in a Heavenly Father?"

More silence followed. But then Albert said softly, "Yes."

I asked, "Why?"

After a pause he spoke again. "Because I was in a car and it went off the road, and just before we crashed I prayed nobody would get hurt, and nobody did."

Soon Roy added that he believed in God because his mother had been sick and he prayed and she got better.

The momentum caused nearly all to join in. Even Jimmy was caught up in the sweet comments being made.

Soon we talked of Jesus. Sadie said, "Jesus is bread and water."

I asked, "Why is that?"

She replied, "Because that is what we have in the sacrament."

I explained about the sacrament, and when I finished she said, "Oh," with understanding.

For several weeks we taught in this way of letting these young people make soul-to-soul comments. Then we had a testimony meeting with all the classes together. There the students took turns expressing their feelings.

At this meeting one would get up and slowly walk up to the front. Incidentally, those students could really walk slowly. All would watch as one made his or her journey to the pulpit. That person would say a few sentences of testimony, and all would watch until he or she had returned to sit down. We spent much of our meeting engaged in travel time.

Finally, toward the end of our time together, on the back row Jimmy stood. Those seeing him stand softly snickered. Jimmy was a clown, and they all laughed a good amount at just about everything he did.

Everyone watched as this strikingly handsome young man in his Levi jacket swaggered his way to the front.

As he held the pulpit with both hands, leaned back, and looked out, a complete silence filled the chapel. All seemed to wonder at once, What funny thing will Jimmy say? I, along with the others, held my breath in anticipation.

After a few seconds our wonder ended as Jimmy's voice rang out. He said, "Something strange is going on up here at LDS seminary. I've been coming up here for three years. In all that time, everything the teacher says goes in this ear [he pointed at his left ear] and comes out here [pointing to his right ear]." Jimmy paused for several seconds.

Finally he spoke again, "But lately a strange thing has been going on. What my teacher says goes in here [again he pointed at his ear], but," he said as he put his hand on his heart, "it has been stopping right here."

There was no laughing. Jimmy the clown was now Jimmy the teacher. As he expressed his feelings about heavenly things, the Spirit of the Lord testified to all of us that what Jimmy said was true.

Joseph Smith Teaches Justice and Mercy

Truman G. Madsen

The Prophet's role as a judge and as mayor of Nauvoo and the head of the Nauvoo Legion required him to discipline the legionnaires and render judgment as the mayor. Anthony, a black, had been selling liquor in violation of the law—to make it worse, on the Sabbath. He pleaded that he needed money urgently to buy the freedom of his child held as a slave in a southern state. Said Joseph: "I am sorry, Anthony, but the law must be observed, and we will have to impose a fine." The next day Joseph gave him a fine horse to purchase the freedom of the child.

The Hunting Trip

John Covey

My father loved hunting with his boys. He made it exciting, building our anticipation with the preparation of the equipment, planning the best locations, and the like. It took weeks of anticipation and effort to finally be ready for the hunt.

I will never forget one Saturday opening of the pheasant hunt. Dad, my older brother, and I were up at 4:00 A.M. We ate Mom's big, hearty breakfast, packed the car, and drove to our designated field by 6:00 A.M. We arrived early to stake out our spot before any others, anticipating the 8:00 A.M. opening hour.

As that hour drew near, other hunters were frantically driving around us, trying to find spots in which to hunt. As seven-forty arrived, we saw hunters driving into the fields. By seven-forty-five the firing had started—fifteen minutes before the official start. We looked at Dad. He made no move except to look at his watch, still waiting for 8:00 A.M. Soon the birds were flying. By seven-fifty all hunters had moved into the fields and shots were everywhere.

Dad looked at his watch. He only said, "The hunt starts at 8:00 A.M., boys." About three minutes before eight, four hunters drove into our spot and walked past us, into our field. We looked at Dad. He said: "The hunt starts for us at eight." At eight the birds were gone, but we started our drive into the field.

We didn't get any birds that day. We did get an unforgettable memory of a man, my ideal, who taught me absolute integrity and whom I fervently wanted to be like.

Courage

"Norman the Mormon"

ALLAN K. BURGESS

The very first Latter-day Saint that Mike ever met was Norman Taylor. He played on a soccer team with Mike and they called him "Norman the Mormon." His honesty and integrity made him unique among the young men on Mike's soccer team. Norman didn't smoke; he didn't drink beer, tea, or coffee; he didn't swear; and he didn't protest any referee's decisions.

One summer, Mike's team reached the English youth cup final for the first time in the team's twenty-five-year history. With less than five minutes to go in the championship game, the score was tied at a goal apiece. The other team was mounting attack after attack. Following a corner kick, the ball bounced off a couple of players and appeared to strike Norman on the hand. The other team immediately appealed for a penalty kick because of the hand-ball violation, while Mike's team denied their appeal.

Both the referee and linesman were unintentionally blocked by players from seeing the incident. The referee, knowing Norman's commitment to honesty and to his beliefs, asked him if he had touched the ball with his hand. Norman quietly answered, "Yes, I did." The referee awarded the other team a penalty kick, which was converted. Moments later the game was over, and Mike's team had lost 2-1.

As the team dejectedly filed into their changing room, not one player said an unkind word or made a scene as Norman sat with his face in his hands, quietly weeping at their loss. "Honesty," he said, "means more to me than anything. I'm sorry—sorry it cost us the game—but I was taught that honesty is a quality that remains with us for life. I can't turn it on and off just for a game."

Mike recollects that he and the team learned a great lesson that day, the lesson that honesty is one of the most valuable of all qualities and that it should always govern our actions, regardless of the cost. Mike later joined the Church and moved to Utah.

The Faith of a Mormon Girl

Elizabeth Claridge McCune

No place on earth seemed so precious to me at fifteen years of age as dear old Nephi. How eagerly we looked forward to the periodical visits of President Brigham Young and his company! Everything was done that could be thought of for their comfort and entertainment. And with all it was a labor of love. One of these visits I shall never forget.

We went out with our Sabbath Schools and all the other organizations, with bands of music and flags and banners and flowers to meet and greet our beloved leader and his company. On this occasion the people were lined up on each side of the street waiting for the carriages to pass. Among them were twenty-five young ladies dressed in white, who had strewn evergreens and wild flowers along the path. Brother Brigham, Brothers Kimball and Wells, with the entire company, got out of their carriages, and walked over the flowery road. When Brother Kimball passed me he said to the group of girls around me, "You five girls right here will live to be mothers in Israel."

The company having been taken to our home, the dinner was served. How we girls flew around to make everything nice for the stylish city folks! As soon as they were seated at dinner, we slipped upstairs and tried on all the ladies' hats. That was a real treat. I venture to say that could the ladies have seen us next Sunday they would have been struck with the similarity of styles in Nephi and city millinery.

We all attended the afternoon meeting, the girls in white having reserved seats in front. The sermons were grand and we were happy until President Young said that he had a few names to read of men who were to be called and voted in as missionaries to go and settle up the "Muddy." This almost stilled the beating of the hearts of all present. Many of our friends had been called to go to settle the Dixie country, but the "Muddy," so many miles farther south and so much worse. Oh! oh! I did not hear another name except Samuel Claridge. Then how I sobbed and cried, regardless of the fact that the tears were spoiling the new white dress. The father of the girl who sat next to me was also called. Said my companion, "Why, what are you crying about? It doesn't make me cry. I know my father won't go." "Well, there is the difference," said I, "I know that my father will go and that nothing could prevent him, and I should not own him as a father if he would not go when he was called." Then I broke down sobbing again.

Everything occurred to prevent my father from getting off. Just as he was nearly ready to start one of his horses got poisoned. He had to buy another horse. A week later one of his big mules was found choked to death in his barn. Some of our friends said, "Brother Claridge, this shows you are not to go." My father answered, "It shows me that the adversary is trying to prevent me from going, but I shall go if I walk!"

As we had just moved into a new house and were fixed comfortably, many of our friends tried to persuade father to keep his home and farm; to go south awhile and then come back. But father knew that this was not the kind of mission upon which he had been called. "I shall sell everything I own," he said, "and take my means to help build up another waste place in Zion."

My mother and sister remained in Nephi the first year, but my brother and myself went with father and his second wife to help make the new home. We packed our wagons with a year's provisions, and, in company with Brother Harmon and wife, started. Thus we traveled, camping at night and cooking our meals over the camp fire to the accompaniment of song and laughter. We were about two weeks in reaching St. George. The Indians in that part of the country were making a great deal of trouble. It was considered unsafe to travel except in large companies. Just previous to our arrival a number of people had been killed, others had their teams stolen by the Indians. The trip from St. George to the Muddy, with loaded teams, required three weeks time. After waiting a week, and no other company coming along, Brother Erastus Snow advised us to go on. Those who have traveled that awful road will recall the loneliness of the scene—the high mountains on either side, the dismal echo of the wagons from wall to wall, which suggested yelling Indians to ears strained to catch the first sound of the red man's war whoop. At night when we camped each man took his turn standing guard. We were under the necessity of traveling a certain number of miles each day, in order to camp where there was water for the animals to drink.

One day I was riding in the wagon with my brother Sam; we were ahead of the others. Several times that day I had made him stop his team because I thought I heard Indians. Each time it proved to be the shrill note of some wild bird. It was now sunset; we could see in the distance our camping place. My brother and I were singing and laughing, when I suddenly heard a yell. "Sam," I said, "Stop the team. I heard the yell of an Indian."

"Yes, you have heard the same yell all day," he answered. I clutched him by the arm.

"Sam, stop! I saw an Indian jump upon the point of that rock and then jump back!" My brother stopped his team. The Indian stood up again and then bounded from one rock to another, followed by two others of his race. We waited until father and Brother Harmon came up to us. By that time ten Indian warriors, all decked out in their war paint were in sight. We stopped and held a solemn consultation. I shall never forget the words of my father and the beautiful expression on his face as he said:

"Don't be afraid, my children! We are in the hands of the Lord! He has called us on this mission. I have done everything in my power to fulfill it so far, and, therefore, our Father will see us through. Go right on; don't let the Indians think you are afraid, for there is nothing an Indian despises so much as cowardice."

We drove right on to the camping place. There we found the Indians already camped. They had a whole band of horses with them, which were evidently the result of their plundering. As we approached they showed no sign of hostility. Father and Brother Harmon fed and watered our horses. Sam made a roaring camp fire. By this time the moon was shining, it seemed to me, as it never shone before. Eleven or twelve of the Indians came over to our camp and squatted peacefully around our fire. This was a sight which is forever riveted on my mind. I thought, "what if my mother and my sweetheart could look through a peepstone and see their loved ones this night!"

Father shook hands with the Indians as they left us; then, after we had our customary evening prayers, we all went quietly to bed. We pretended to sleep that night, but I think not one closed his eyes. I remember well the feeling of gratitude which came into my heart when I thought, "What a good man my father is; our safety is due to his goodness and to the righteousness of Brother Harmon." They were both pure men and faithful Latter-day Saints. I felt secure as I reflected that these two good men held that power which is the Priesthood of God.

1,300 Degrees Fahrenheit

Marion D. Hanks

During the second World War, the first great B-29 strike on those who were then our enemy, flown from a land base, was led by an airplane named "City of Los Angeles." (There had been previous strikes from carriers, but this was our first flown from our own airfields recovered from the enemy. It was meant to inform him that the war was now to be carried to his own homeland, and it was a very important mission.) Aboard the aircraft were twelve men, eleven regular crewmen and a colonel flying as squadron commander for the mission. They were to reach a rendezvous point fifty to seventy-five miles off the mainland of the enemy, then assume regular fighting formation and fly in on target, which was a complex of high-octane gasoline plants feeding the enemy war potential.

Rendezvous point was reached as scheduled, and Colonel Sprouse ordered the dropping of the phosphorous bomb which was to mark the point. Sergeant "Red" Irwin skidded the bomb down the chute as ordered. The act was loaded with death. The flap at the end of the bomb chute had somehow become stuck. When the bomb struck it, it exploded prematurely and burst back into the cabin of the airplane and into the face and chest of Sergeant Irwin. Dropping to the deck, it began swiftly to burn its way through the thin metal flooring separating it from the incendiary bombs stored in the bomb bay below. In moments the "City of Los Angeles" and its crew would be blown to bits far out over the ocean in enemy territory.

Sergeant Irwin, tragically wounded, got to his knees, picked up the bomb in his bare hands, cradled it in his arms, and staggered up the passageway. Crashing into the navigator's table, he had to stop and unlatch it with fingers that left burn marks in the hardwood. By now the aircraft was filled with acrid fumes, blinding the pilot, and was wallowing less than three hundred feet above the water. Irwin staggered into the pilot's compartment shouting, "Window, window." He could not see that it was already open, and his fumbling fingers left burn marks on the metal. He threw the bomb out of the window and collapsed to the deck. Two hours later, Colonel Sprouse having ordered the "City of Los Angeles" back to base in the slim hope that Irwin's life might be saved, they reached Iwo Jima. Irwin's flesh was still smoking with imbedded phosphorous when he was removed from the plane by comrades who had to avert their faces from his tragic wounds.

Sergeant Irwin lived to receive his nation's highest honor for extreme bravery and to survive nearly fifty plastic surgery operations which restored him to a somewhat normal life. He lived to marry and to become a father. And with him there lived eleven other men who, but for his almost unbelievable courage, would be dead. Eleven men, spared to their lives and work and families through the decision and courageous act of one man! When Sergeant Irwin picked up that bomb, he knew that it was burning at 1,300 degrees Fahrenheit, 1,088 degrees hotter than boiling water!

This dramatic story came out of a war, but its implications are applicable to each of us, to our families, communities, nations. How many young people are there in your home or neighborhood, choice young children of God, who are wanting for lack of someone who has the courage and concern to interest himself or herself in their welfare?

Rock-Throwing Lessons

KEVIN STOKER

Late in 1955, Elder Roger Beitler and his companion met stiff opposition as they tried to open the Brazilian city of Piracicaba to missionary work. Every day for a month, a local religious leader used his afternoon radio program to preach against the Mormons. But this anti-Mormon fervor would soon provide an opportunity for Elder Beitler, serving in only his first area, to hurl the work forward in a remarkable way.

The missionaries had spent most of their time proselyting with little success in the center of Piracicaba. Hoping that people in another area might be more receptive, they boarded a bus bound for the south end of the city. The bus line ended in a *praca* (square) next to a large Catholic church. The missionaries stepped off the bus at about the same time several padres came out of the church. The padres, who had just finished their monthly meeting, stopped and stared at the two Americans. "In those days," Elder Beitler recalls, "the missionaries were required to wear hats, and I had a beautiful white Panama. I doffed my hat and said, 'Good morning, fathers.' They all twirled around and rushed back into the church."

The elders continued down a hill and began knocking on doors in a new residential area. As the missionaries went from door to door, they were followed by an increasing number of children. A lady, calling herself a believer (Protestant), invited the elders in for a drink of water. She was kind, but not too interested in their message. They were about to leave, when a loud commotion outside caused the lady to look out the window. She gasped and advised them to stay. Waiting to confront the missionaries was an unruly mob that now included more adults than children. At the head of the crowd was a padre wearing a long, black robe.

"We decided we couldn't hide there all day, so we walked out the door and were met with shouts of derision," Elder Beitler remembers. His companion warned him to stay at his side and then walked toward the padre. The padre and the mob retreated before the missionaries. The companion smiled, then took off his hat and said, "Good morning, father. May I help you?" When the padre could back up no further, he replied, "Yes, you can help me. You can help me by leaving this area and never coming back." The elders continued to smile as they slowly turned around and headed up the hill toward the bus stop. Moments later, Elder Beitler heard the sound of something whizzing through the air and clattering against the street.

"We're being stoned," he thought. "I can't believe it. They stoned Stephen! They stoned Paul! And now I, Roger Beitler, am being stoned."

His euphoria and exhilaration ended abruptly when a rock struck him hard in the shoulder. Whipping his six-foot-two, two-hundred-pound frame around, he picked up a rock, and reared back to throw it at the padre leading the group. "Not a person moved. Not a sound was made. I had that rock in my hand, and I weighed it, up and down, flexing my fingers around it, all the time looking that padre straight in the eye." The young missionary, a former semipro baseball pitcher, had no doubt he could strike his target. "But," he thought, "I haven't come all the way to Brazil to throw rocks at people. I'm here to teach the gospel."

About one hundred feet away, he spied a metal utility pole and fired the rock into the pole. "Waannng!" The metal shuddered at the impact.

"No music was ever sweeter to my ears," he recalls. "The people ceased to be a mob and now became spectators." One of the boys in the crowd threw a rock at the pole, missing it by a long distance. Then, others in the crowd began hurling rocks wildly at the pole, but not one struck the metal. The elders also began throwing rocks at the pole, hitting it several times before picking up their hats and leaving without incident.

The next day, when the missionaries returned to the area,

they were met by several boys who asked if they would teach them how to throw rocks. After that, a pile of rocks was waiting for the missionaries whenever they were in the area. "Pretty soon, when we came to the doors of people in the area, the parents would say. 'You must be the Americans who know how to throw rocks; I've been curious about you, come in.' And for the first time, missionary work progressed in that town."

Twenty years later, in 1975, President Roger Beitler of the Brazil Sao Paulo South Mission interviewed a missionary, who happened to be from the Piracicaba Ward. President Beitler asked where the meetinghouse was located. "You know where the *praca* is on the south side of town, across the river?" the elder said. "You go down the hill from the Catholic church, and where [the area] flattens out . . . , we now have one of the most beautiful chapels in all of Brazil."

Richard Kirkland, the Humane Hero of Fredericksburg

General J. B. Kershaw

Editor's Note: The Civil War soldier who is the subject of this story, Richard Rowland Kirkland, has come to be known as the "Angel of Marye's Heights" (Marye's Heights being the landmark near which Kirkland's unit was positioned). A beautiful monument honoring his courageous and merciful actions now stands at the site of the battle of Fredericksburg in Virginia. The author of the story, General J. B. Kershaw, was Kirkland's brigade commander and is the general referred to in the following account.

214

Richard Kirkland was the son of John Kirkland, an estimable citizen of Kershaw county, a plain, substantial farmer of the olden time. In 1861 he entered as a private Captain J. D. Kennedy's company (E) of the Second South Carolina volunteers, in which company he was a sergeant in December, 1862.

The day after the sanguinary battle of Fredericksburg, Kershaw's brigade occupied the road at the foot of Marye's hill and the ground about Marye's house, the scene of their desperate defence of the day before. One hundred and fifty yards in front of the road, the stone facing of which constituted the famous stone wall, lay Syke's division of regulars, U.S.A., between whom and our troops a murderous skirmish occupied the whole day, fatal to many who heedlessly exposed themselves, even for a moment. The ground between the lines was bridged with the wounded, dead and dying Federals, victims of the many desperate and gallant assaults of that column of 30,000 brave men hurled vainly against that impregnable position.

All that day those wounded men rent the air with their groans and their agonizing cries of "Water! water!" In the afternoon the General sat in the north room, up stairs, of Mrs. Stevens' house, in front of the road, surveying the field, when Kirkland came up. With an expression of indignant remonstrance pervading his person, his manner and the tone of his voice, he said, "General! I can't stand this."

"What is the matter, Sergeant?" asked the General.

He replied, "All night and all day I have heard those poor people crying for water, and I can stand it no longer. I come to ask permission to go and give them water."

The General regarded him for a moment with feelings of profound admiration, and said: "Kirkland, don't you know that you would get a bullet through your head the moment you stepped over the wall?"

"Yes, sir," he said, "I know that; but if you will let me, I am willing to try it."

After a pause, the General said, "Kirkland, I ought not to allow you to run a risk, but the sentiment which actuates you is so noble that I will not refuse your request, trusting that God may protect you. You may go."

The Sergeant's eye lighted up with pleasure. He said, "Thank you, sir," and ran rapidly down stairs. The General heard him pause for a moment, and then return, bounding two steps at a time. He thought the Sergeant's heart had failed him. He was mistaken. The Sergeant stopped at the door and said: "General, can I show a white handkerchief?" The General slowly shook his head, saying emphatically, "No, Kirkland, you can't do that." "All right," he said, "I'll take the chances," and ran down with a bright smile on his handsome countenance.

With profound anxiety he was watched as he stepped over the wall on his errand of mercy—Christ-like mercy. Unharmed he reached the nearest sufferer. He knelt beside him, tenderly raised the drooping head, rested it gently upon his own noble breast, and poured the precious life-giving fluid down the fever-scorched throat. This done, he laid him tenderly down, placed his knap-sack under his head, straightened out his broken limb, spread his overcoat over him, replaced his empty canteen with a full one, and turned to another sufferer. By this time his purpose was well understood on both sides, and all danger was over. From all parts of the field arose fresh cries of "Water, water; for God's sake, water!" More piteous still the mute appeal of some who could only feebly lift a hand to say, here, too, is life and suffering.

For an hour and a half did this ministering angel pursue his labor of mercy, nor ceased to go and return until he relieved all the wounded on that part of the field. He returned to his post wholly unhurt. Who shall say how sweet his rest that winter's night beneath the cold stars!

Little remains to be told. Sergeant Kirkland distinguished himself in battle at Gettysburg, and was promoted lieutenant. At Chickamauga he fell on the field of battle, in the hour of victory. He was but a youth when called away, and had never formed those ties from which might have resulted in a posterity to enjoy his fame and bless his country; but he has bequeathed to the American youth—yea, to the world—an example which dignifies our common humanity.

$\mathscr{P}$rayers of Courage

ANITA R. CANFIELD

O ne year ago we learned that our son had a life-threatening heart problem. He had been experiencing an extreme rapid heartbeat after exertion for the past two years. We had seen doctors, and he had been tested. The diagnosis was that he had a non-life-threatening ailment that we were told he would eventually outgrow. When a notable sports figure dropped dead because of a similar condition, our concern multiplied as we read about the symptoms this man had before he died. They seemed to be closely related to what our son was experiencing.

We decided to take him to a medical center that specialized in the heart. The day before we went in for his testing, his father gave him a blessing in which he was promised he would be made whole. A tremendous witness was given to us during the blessing; a spiritual experience of comfort.

The next day we learned that his condition was an unusual case of a rare type of ventricular tachycardia. We were told it was life threatening and inoperable. His heart was aging prematurely, and the best we could hope for was a pacemaker by the time he was twenty. We were told, with the rapid advances in technology, time would hopefully be on his side. His life would now be severely restricted. He could not participate in any sports or physical activity or go above altitudes of five thousand feet or below ten feet of water.

I stayed with him that night in the hospital while my husband flew back to Las Vegas. That evening we spoke by phone. He asked, "But what about the blessing, what did all that mean?" I could feel his sorrow. But the witness during the blessing had been real. We knew we had to exercise our faith. That blessing was from the Lord. We felt it. Maybe the procedure that would make Chase whole again hadn't been invented yet. We had to believe in that blessing.

Early the next morning one of the doctors came to the room. He said he had not been able to get Chase off his mind and that morning he had taken the case to the weekly breakfast meeting of all the heart surgeons. They had reviewed the data and the diagnosis. He told us that there was a new procedure that was done only by three or four doctors in the entire country. They did not do it at their facility. The closest facility that performed the procedure was at the University of California in San Francisco. The doctor told us it was the unanimous opinion of the group that morning that we should investigate this procedure and see if our son was a candidate for it.

After a visit to the surgeon in San Francisco and still more tests, it was determined that Chase was indeed a candidate for the surgery. He was given a medication that would control the attacks, and a surgery date was scheduled four months from that time. We were told the procedure was only eighteen months old but the results were statistically excellent. There were no guarantees, but we were filled with new hope.

Within six weeks he began having breakthroughs in the medication. The arrhythmias were starting again. The medicine wasn't working. The surgery was immediately scheduled for the following Monday morning.

Chase, who had been seemingly nonchalant until this point, began to grow obviously nervous and afraid. No matter what we said, he seemed to grow more uncertain, more concerned about never returning home. Our ward held a special fast. That Sunday evening friends and family gathered in our home and knelt in prayer as the bishop prayed and asked the Lord to accept our offering.

We watched and felt an overpowering spirit of peace engulf the room, and especially Chase. With a trembling voice, he expressed his gratitude and love for their efforts in his behalf.

We boarded the plane that night, and he told me that no matter what happened he would always remember that sacred experience in our home. He said during the prayer he felt

God's love for him, for the Saints, and for his family. He felt peace and he said he felt power, even power to overcome his fear and his great trial that lay in the path of his life. No matter what happened, he would never forget.

The surgery went well we were told, in fact, faster than they expected. That evening, in his hospital room, eight hours after surgery, he lay in his bed, foggy and struggling to recover from the anesthesia. He was sick and crying out in pain. The nurses kept trying in vain to make him comfortable. He was completely unaware of his surroundings and began to grow clammy and cold.

After standing by watching him struggle for several hours, he seemed to be getting worse. Unable to stand the uncertainty and panic for another moment, I quickly asked that a doctor immediately come examine him. Within minutes of the doctor's arrival, Chase was seized by another attack. Our hopes were dashed as we realized that the operation had not been successful at all. I felt paralyzed as I saw his blood pressure plummet on the monitor. As if in a nightmare, I heard the words *code blue* over the loudspeaker and watched, horrified, as doctors and nurses rushed into the room.

We were forced to stand outside in the hall, feeling utterly helpless, numbly watching the medical team work frantically to save his life. I wrapped spiritual arms around a rod of faith, witness, testimony, and prayers for the life of my son.

Standing in the hostility of that stark, white, lonely hall, my eyes frantically searched to find some part of him, some indication of life, the blush of his skin, but all I could find was his face white as a sheet, punctuating the chaos around his bed. If he was about to die, I wanted it to be in my arms and not under the cold, sterile hands of strangers. I was with him when he came into the world, I wanted to be with him and breathe with him his last breath if this was his time to leave.

All at once I was overcome with a new feeling. I felt as if that once lonely hallway was suddenly filled with friends and family, even my entire ward, comforting me and sustaining me with their prayers. I was encouraged and began again to remember.

Many things that I needed to remember suddenly rushed into my mind: blessings, spiritual experiences, and whole verses of scriptures all brought me comfort. I was renewed as a peace began to wash over me and swell within me.

The Lord spared Chase's life. He spent the night in the intensive care unit. The next day the doctors expressed their desire to try again. They explained that they believed they had only stunned the area with the laser and had not destroyed the diseased cells. They knew where the cells were, even the exact spot. They believed that Chase had been so anesthetized that the area appeared clear when actually it had been only "stunned." They wanted to proceed again. However, there was one small catch. Chase would have to remain awake as long as possible in order for them to be absolutely certain they were successful. This had to be his choice.

He looked at us with a conviction in his eyes, and said, "I can do it. I remember the blessing, the fast, the prayers. I want to try again. I know Heavenly Father will help me."

The surgery took six and one-half hours. He was given no anesthetic. We were told they were successful in destroying all the diseased cells. When he was returned to the room one of the doctors personally pushed the gurney and helped the nurse gently get him into bed. He expressed to us his admiration for Chase's character and told us that he had been deeply touched and affected by his courage. As the doctor and nurses left the room, finally leaving us alone together, Chase began to weep, unable to restrain the tears any longer. Then the words came; unable to restrain his emotions, he told us of the incredible spiritual experiences that he had during those grueling six and one-half hours of surgery.

They had given him a little anesthetic in the beginning to get the shunts into his arteries and up into his heart. For about the first twenty minutes he was okay. Then he began to feel the pain and the hideous sensation of the catheters in his heart. He heard the noises, listened to the dialogue of the medical team, felt the burning, smelled the nauseating antiseptic odors. Anxiety began to creep over him and he began to fall deeper and deeper into the clutches of fear. He wept and begged, "Please, please, you have to give me something." The doctor operating the catheter asked him to please hang on twenty or thirty more minutes so they could be more certain of success. Chase closed his eyes and began to pray silently, pleading for help. Suddenly, he remembered again the prayers, the blessing. As he lay thinking and meditating upon those words, he began to hear voices. He listened carefully and realized that he was hearing people praying for him. Calmness returned like a strange force, and he was able to go on for the next thirty minutes.

Then he began to feel more pain, and all his physical senses began again to be acutely aware of what was happening. He cried out for relief. Again, the doctor asked for more time. Just ten or fifteen minutes more they wanted. He prayed for strength, and again he heard people praying for him. He began to listen, this time concentrating on the voices. During the hours that followed this was how he overcame fear and panic. Just when he felt he could bear no more, the prayers would come to his mind. He began to hear and distinguish familiar voices. He said, "Mom, I heard you. This is what you said . . ." and he repeated to me the exact words and sentences I had prayed for him over the previous months and in the hours in the hospital. He said, "Dad, I heard you, and this is what you said. . . ." Again, he repeated Steve's exact words to the Lord. His uncle, aunt, and grandparents called, and he shared the same experience with them. That day of remembering will be with us all as the future unfolds more trials and tribulations. We can endure to the end. These memories and others like them, provide us with the ability to grip harder in the dark the rod we have seen only in the light.

$\mathcal{I}$f It Is to Be It Is Up to Me

George D. Durrant

I recall being called to Kentucky and Tennessee as a mission president. My son Matt was at the time a ninth-grader in a Salt Lake City school. There he had made many friends and had enjoyed an excellent social life. His keen sense of humor and other characteristics had helped him find satisfaction at school. It was my lot to advise him that this pleasant life with its comfortable environment was to change.

I chose as the place for this news conference with my son a local restaurant—a place where you could go through the line and get all the food you wanted. After we had gone through the line and were sitting at the table, the only way I could see him was to look around the masses of food that balanced precariously on his plate.

After our prayer, and just as he started to eat, I broke the news. He was of course shocked, but as he swallowed the food he was eating, he said: "I'm ready to go, Dad. I'm proud of you, and I'll do my best." I don't think he realized then, and nor did I, how difficult the years ahead would be for him.

We arrived in Kentucky just in time for him to start his sophomore year in the largest school in the state. His only acquaintances were three or four other Mormon young people whom he had met a week or so earlier in church. As the first few weeks passed by he got right into his studies, and his grades appeared to be excellent. But his social life suffered. He didn't feel that he belonged there. He had no real friends. Although he didn't discuss this with me, he spent many, many anxious days wishing he was back with his old friends.

He became depressed. But he had hope, because it would soon be time for the basketball team to be chosen. He was certain that this would be the doorway to happiness. He made the junior varsity team but often found himself seated on the bench. Although he was good, he was not yet as good as he had dreamed he might be. So basketball, his last hope, was not giving him the satisfaction he needed. His sophomore year was not a happy one.

Then came the beginning of his junior year. He had grown considerably and had practiced basketball all summer. Many at the school had gained respect for him because of his straight "A" grades, an unusual thing on that particular basketball team. He had some satisfaction in that, but he wanted satisfaction along different lines. He wanted social satisfaction and athletic satisfaction. He felt that he had to prove himself. To him, the place to do that was on the basketball court.

The time came for the varsity team to be chosen. He had played well and was hoping to be on the main five. He enthusiastically entered the gymnasium to look at that all-important list posted by the coach. He stood with others looking at the names. He read from top to bottom. His name was not on the list at all. He had been cut from the team. In his mind that meant he had been cut from everything.

He returned home that day before school was out, went to his room and stayed there. I knew of the deep grief he was suffering but didn't know how to help. On the second day of his sorrows, late at night I went downstairs to his room. His light was still on and he was looking up at the ceiling from his position lying on the bed. We talked. We talked for a long time. He told me of his deep sorrow and wondered if he could ever return to school. He told me that he had prayed and asked the Lord to help him make the team. And now he said, "I've prayed for strength." But there seemed to be no help and there seemed to be no hope. I thought my heart would break as I saw my son suffer. I listened, I loved, and I silently prayed.

After a while he said to me: "Dad, I'm just going to have to start over. I'm going to have to build on something else. I know no one else can do it for me. I've got to do it for myself." With tear-filled eyes he said to me, "Dad, I want to be like Elder Jibson and I think I can be." He had named one of the elders who was serving in the mission. He continued: "I'm going to be like him. I'm going to learn to smile like him, and to love and care like him. Dad, I'm going to make it. I'm going back to school and I'm going to start over." We knelt in prayer together, and then I told him of my love for him and of the great pride I had in him.

The next day he went to school. During that season he played basketball for the church team, where he was a star. He started to make many friends at school. He seemed to be relaxed, and he returned to and further developed his keen sense of humor. As time went by I heard him saying such things as: "Dad, these guys are great! I love this school. I love this town and I love Kentucky. I even wonder if after our mission we could live here."

The beginning of his senior year arrived. Because of some difficulties in the school system they had not yet elected the student body president for the year. He decided to run for president. By now he had many friends. He carried on a great campaign based on positive, fun-loving things about how he could help the school to be a better place. He was elected by a landslide. Of course, he was thrilled.

But there was one last dream at his school and that was something he hadn't been able to get out of his system. He wanted to be on the basketball team. The coach had announced that he wouldn't carry any seniors who hadn't played as juniors. Instead he wanted juniors on the team who could help him in the future. Thus there seemed to be no hope for Matt, who was a senior. Nevertheless he practiced long and hard, and the guys who were the stars on the team came to love and respect him.

When the list was posted, once again his name did not appear. As much as he had tried to build himself in other directions, he was again heartbroken. He came home and told me of his problems. At the time I was just departing on a journey and I wouldn't return for five days. All that I could do while I was gone was pray.

When I got back I found that Matt was not home. He was at basketball practice. I inquired if he was practicing with the church and I was told that he was practicing with the school. About that time he arrived home. "How come you practice with the team?" I asked. "You told me you were cut."

"Well, Dad," he replied, "the guys on the team all went to the coach and told him they wanted me on the team. The coach did something he'd never done before. He put me on the team because the guys said, 'We need Mat.' They convinced the coach, so I'm on the team."

He continued his friendly ways. School was composed of both blacks and whites. He befriended them all. He became a great influence in the school—to help unify it, to help all to have more pride in it. On one occasion in a senior class meeting there arose a division among the black students and the white students over who should play the music at the last dance. The blacks wanted a black group and the whites wanted a certain white group. Some of the more vocal groups of both factions began to shout, and a potential little riot seemed to be shaping up. Matt got the microphone.

"Quiet, quiet," he said. And then when there was silence he continued. "I have a solution. There's a group up in Cincinnati we can get. It's five Chinese guys."

His announcement was first met with silence, but then came a unanimous burst of laughter. Tempers cooled and a sensible discussion followed.

Matt and the other Mormon kids, as a group, set a great example at that school. A Mormon girl became vice president and she was also named Miss Seneca, the highest honor the school could bestow upon a young lady.

Matt still felt bad about basketball because he was usually on the bench. One night at a team meeting the projector broke down and game films could not be shown as planned. The team and the coach just sat around and talked. Matt sort of entertained the group. For the first time the coach really found out who Matt was. In the next game he played for over half the game. From then on he was a major factor in many games and gained recognition as a superior athlete.

Finally it was graduation time. He was chosen to give one of the talks. The humor in the talk caused a good deal of laughter. But it was also a serious talk. Toward the conclusion of his remarks, he spoke of the joy he had known there—the warmth of the people, the love he had for the other students. He closed by saying: "My dear friends, in a few days my parents and I will be returning to Utah. As you know, I am a Mormon. I conclude my remarks by using the unforgettable words of a great Mormon prophet Brigham Young. His words describe my feeling. I love all of you because of the way you've treated me and the happiness and joy I've had here. And so I say to you, as he once said, "This is the place." The students and the public rose to their feet and gave him a standing ovation.

Matt had made many steps toward his destiny, a journey which started in a quiet room where, after a trial of his faith, he made a decision to start over, a decision which could be paraphrased by the words, "If it is to be it is up to me." He had decided to build first upon the idea of reaching his destiny as a special person. As he did that, other things fell into place.

His Own Mind

MARION D. HANKS

The young Mormon marine was uneasy and didn't know why. There were plenty of ordinary reasons for a member of a combat unit in almost daily contact with the enemy to feel uneasy, but this was something different. When he returned with his group to their base camp after several days in the field, he discovered what it was.

"C'mon, Smith," the sergeant said. "The whole outfit's going into town. This time you're coming with us even if we have to drag you. You are about to find out how big men live when they get away from their mamas."

Rick Smith caught the sharp edge of the other's voice, knifing through the seeming lightness of his words. He understood the look in the eye and the tightness at the corners of the mouth. Sarge wasn't kidding; he really intended to take Rick along, even if he had to drag him.

"No thanks, Sarge," Rick said. "I'm staying here."

"Listen, Sonny," came the grim answer, "big men can make up their own minds about their lives. They don't stay tied to Mommy's apron strings when they're in this man's outfit. You're coming with us."

Rick Smith could feel the color drain from his face and the strength ebb from his knees, but his voice surprised him with its calmness as he heard himself answer:

"You're right, Sarge, a big man can make up his own mind. I have the responsibility to decide whether I'll live the way you do or the way I believe in. You've made *your* choice, Sergeant, and that's your business. But I still have a choice, and I prefer to live another way. That's what I've made up my mind to do. I'm staying here."

The sergeant turned on his heel, muttering curses. Elder Richard Smith, nineteen, found a quiet place, and in his loneliness he thanked God in his heart for an answer he had been afraid he might not know how to give. He'd been uneasy because he had somehow known intuitively that there was a different kind of battle ahead of him that day. He was sure now that there were more battles to come, but he'd won this one, and he was grateful.

Happiness
and
Gratitude

$\mathscr{B}$ecause I Have Been Given Much

RICHARD M. SIDDOWAY

I questioned why the Jenkins family bought the old Whipple home as much as anyone. Four or five years before, Virginia Jenkins had suffered a stroke that left her confined to a wheelchair and without speech. The Whipple home had five bedrooms on its two floors and a large yard that required constant care. The Jenkinses were both in their seventies when they moved in. It seemed to me to be too large for their needs. But move in they did.

Patrick Jenkins stood over six feet tall. He had a thatch of snow white hair that seemed always to be falling forward over his left eye. He stood ramrod straight and spoke in quick, clipped words. His standard outfit consisted of a blue workshirt, sleeves rolled to the elbows, and a pair of well-worn overalls. The day they moved in he began constructing a ramp to the front door. He worked with the speed and skill of a practiced carpenter. By evening he was able to wheel his wife up the ramp and into their living room.

Virginia Jenkins sat strapped to her wheelchair. Although she could not speak, she obviously understood everything that was going on. She had lost the use of her left arm, but her right hand was constantly in motion, pointing to one thing or another in the room. She and her husband seemed to communicate without words, or at least without words from her. Patrick was always chatting away. "Well, Mother, I think we've fixed this ramp up pretty good. What do you think? Let's give it a try. Grab on, Mother, and we'll try to keep from bucking you out." And up the ramp they went.

When they moved in, a huge number of people showed up to help them. I offered a hand if it was needed, but Patrick said, "I think we have everything pretty much under control, don't we, Mother! But thanks for your offer."

"Your family?" I asked indicating the army of helpers.

He paused for a minute and surveyed the crew. "Yes . . . our family."

Within a week the whole neighborhood was familiar with the Jenkinses' routine. At eight o'clock every morning the front door opened and out came Virginia Jenkins in her wheelchair. Patrick pushed her down the ramp and around the house to the backyard. There he parked her in the shade of a huge chestnut tree while he worked in the garden. Every few minutes he came to her side and asked if she needed anything. Usually she shook her head, but occasionally she nodded her head and then Patrick began his guessing game. "Do you want a drink, Mother?" She'd either shake or nod her head. If he was wrong, Patrick continued, "Are you hungry, Mother? Do you need to be moved? Are you too cold? Are you too hot?" On and on he'd go until he guessed Virginia's need.

Throughout the week various members of the family appeared at their home. From my vantage point across the street, I began to recognize some of their children. Three or four times a week a blue Honda pulled up and a dark-complexioned woman of considerable bulk climbed out. She'd walk around the house to the back yard and spend a few minutes before she reappeared, climbed into her little car, and drove away. Not quite so frequently a bright red Chevrolet pulled up and a short, blond woman with two small children emerged.

The Jenkinses had a garden area in their back yard about forty feet square. The Whipples had not planted anything in it for several years. One Saturday morning I watched Patrick push Virginia around the house and a few minutes later saw him carry an armload of weeds to the garbage can on the curb. I walked across the road and into their backyard. Virginia sat in the shade of the chestnut tree while Patrick sliced away at the weed patch with a scythe. When he spotted me, he laid his scythe against the fence and walked toward me. He pulled off his leather work glove and shook my hand. "What a pleasure to have you visit Mother and me," he said. "It will give me a well-needed break." Virginia smiled at me and waved her right hand. I took it in mine and shook it gently. She squeezed my hand firmly.

"I have a tiller," I said. "Could I be of assistance? I'd be happy to till that garden area for you."

Virginia's face lit up. Patrick said, "Are you sure? I wouldn't want to be a burden to you."

"I'll go get it and we'll turn those weeds under for you." I returned a few minutes later with the tiller. The ground was fairly hard and hadn't been tilled for several years. We bounced merrily around with the tiller without doing much harm to the ground. "Why don't we put the water on it for a little while and I'll come back this afternoon and turn it under," I suggested.

Patrick nodded, and turned on the sprinklers that covered the garden area. "I really don't want to take all your time," he said.

"No problem. Just leave the water on for an hour or so and I'll come back later." I wheeled the tiller back home.

Later that afternoon I returned to the Jenkinses' backyard. As soon as I started the tiller, Patrick came out the back door. "Can you wait for a minute?" he asked. "Mother would like to see this." I waited until he wheeled his wife around the corner of the house and adjusted her in the shade beneath the chestnut tree. I started the tiller and began turning over the garden area. An hour later I'd made a couple of passes in each direction. The garden looked much better. I started home.

"Wait!" called Patrick over the sound of the motor. "Mother wants to thank you." He motioned me over to his wife's chair. I stopped the tiller and walked over to Virginia. She reached up with her good hand, squeezed mine, and patted me on the arm. Her face beamed a radiant smile. "We don't know how to repay you," said Patrick.

"Happy to do it," I said, and started home with my tiller.

The next morning in church Virginia squeezed my arm and

smiled into my face. Patrick thanked me for all of the work in his yard.

The following Saturday I walked over to the Jenkinses' home again. Although it was fairly late in the season to plant a garden, Patrick had planted rows of tomato plants, beans, peppers, cucumbers, and lettuce. "Had to put in container-grown ones this year," he said. "Next year I'm going to start my own. Mother and I are going to build a little greenhouse in the basement workroom." He paused. "Oh, by the way, I noticed your tiller was running a little rough last week. I hope you don't mind, but I tuned it up for you."

"Not at all, I appreciate it," I said. When I got home I looked at my tiller. Every speck of dirt had been wiped from it, the rust spots had been painted over, and it sported a new set of tines. I pulled the starter rope. It started on the first pull and ran better than it had in years.

A few mornings later a crew of ten or twelve men appeared outside the Jenkinses' home. By the time they left that evening the entire outside of the house had been painted. The siding shone bright white. The murky olive trim had been painted forest green.

"Your house looks marvellous," I said to Patrick the next morning.

"Mother's happy with it." He indicated Virginia sitting beneath the chestnut tree. "Our boys did a good job."

"Were all of those men your sons?" I asked.

"Our family," he smiled. Virginia nodded happily.

By the end of the summer the Jenkinses' garden was yielding produce by the bushel. Every plant had been individually tended by Patrick. No weeds grew in his hand-groomed garden. Two or three times a week Patrick waited for the blue Honda to pull up. Then he filled his garden cart with tomatoes and cucumbers and left Virginia to her daughter's care while he walked through the neighborhood distributing vegetables from his cart.

Frost finally came. I turned their garden under with our tiller. As the weather grew colder, Patrick no longer pushed Virginia out beneath the tree each day. When I came home from work I'd look at the picture window in their front room. Often Virginia was sitting there. I'd wave and she'd return my wave.

Thanksgiving morning dawned bright, clear, and cold. Early in the morning the cars began to arrive across the street. By ten o'clock, well over a dozen were parked in their driveway and on the street. The phone rang. It was Patrick. "I don't want to bother you on this Thanksgiving Day, but do you by chance have any folding chairs we could borrow? We thought we'd borrowed enough from the church, but we've come up about six short."

"We've got eight of them," I replied. "I'll bring them over."

"Oh," he said, "the boys and I can come and get them. We don't want to put you out."

I had carried four of the chairs onto the front porch, when two young men approached from across the street. I couldn't help notice how different they looked from each other. One was a tall, skinny blond with piercing blue eyes. The other was short, and dark enough to have been Polynesian. We carried the chairs to the Jenkinses' home. Patrick had not only been working on the outside of the home but been remodeling the inside of the house as well. A wall had been removed and an enormous dining room created. In that room were nearly four dozen people, with Virginia seated at one end of the table in her wheelchair, and Patrick at the other. There were people with red, blond, brunette, and black hair. Their skin tones ran from white to chocolate. Patrick leapt to his feet, his eyes glistening. "Family, our good friend and neighbor." He put his arm around my shoulders. Then, indicating the others, he said, "My family. No. Our family." He beamed at his wife. There were greetings from the group mingled with Patrick's effusive thanks for the chairs.

I turned to go. Patrick said, "Wait just a moment. Mother has been working very hard these past few weeks." The room grew silent. All eyes turned toward Virginia. She smiled. Then a look of enormous concentration appeared on her face. Her lips tensed, and with great effort she said, "Dhang you fo' gummin'."

She relaxed and smiled. Patrick beamed while we all applauded.

That evening as Patrick and I carried the chairs back to my home, he said, "That was probably quite a shock to you, meeting our family all at one time."

"Just a little confusing, is more like it."

Patrick sank into the couch in my living room. "Mother and I have never been able to have any children of our own," he began. "So we just helped raise kids that nobody else wanted. Some of them came from racially mixed parentage. Some were crippled or handicapped in some way. Mother just raised them as if they were her own. Not all of them have turned out as well as we'd hoped, but most have. I think nearly everybody responds to love and kindness, don't you?"

I nodded.

"About fifteen years ago Mother had her first stroke," Patrick continued. "I realized we probably couldn't continue taking in any more kids. It just about killed her. But our children—and they really are our children, you know—have been so good. They come by and check on us. We've tried to be as independent as we can, but it's still good to know someone cares. They give Mother a reason to live and to keep trying to recover. She worked so hard to be able to greet our family." His eyes brimmed with tears. "I've got to get home to her. She's a real treasure, my boy."

The following Sunday was the first one in December, which meant we would be having a fast and testimony meeting at church. After the opening hymn and prayer, a baby was blessed. The sacrament was passed, and then it was time for testimony bearing. Patrick Jenkins pushed his wife's wheelchair to the front of the chapel. He picked up the microphone that had been used by the father who had blessed his son. "My dear brothers and sisters," began Patrick, "my wife and I have lived in this ward for over six months, and in that time we've never taken advantage of the opportunity to bear our testimonies." He brushed his white hair back from his forehead. "You have taken us in and made us feel so welcome. My dear wife has trouble speaking, as you know, but she would like to say something to you today." He placed the microphone in front of Virginia's lips.

The room grew quiet as she struggled for a moment and then said, "Read!" She smiled.

Patrick said very quietly, "She would like me to read two of her favorite hymns. They express her testimony. Please follow with us 'I Know That My Redeemer Lives' and 'Count Your Blessings.'" No one made a sound as Patrick Jenkins read the message of these two hymns. Nor was there any question that she believed what he read. She indeed, wheelchair-bound and all, felt herself truly blessed. Patrick wheeled his wife back to his seat.

She died before the winter snows melted. Patrick continued to tend the garden that spring and summer, but the spring was gone from his step. "I never got her greenhouse built," he said humbly. "She did so like to see things grow." He joined her before Thanksgiving.

"*I* Feel Sorry for Him"

JOHN H. GROBERG

Editor's Note: In the 1950s Elder John H. Groberg served a mission on the islands of Tonga. As time went on and he served the Lord willingly on these isles of the sea, he became more aware of the villagers' physical poverty and their constant struggles with death, illness, and wild hurricanes. At times, the routine of island life could be monotonous. But many times the light of humble spirits shone brightly, making the islands the most blessed place on earth.

Then, one day, new excitement! A strange boat was working its way into the harbor. Hurray for something different! The whole island was soon down to the seashore looking at one of the most beautiful sailing yachts I have ever seen.

Quietly, as if in slow motion, a crewman threw an anchor into the waiting lagoon. It did not even appear to make a splash, as though to refrain from disturbing the beauty of the scene. It was nearly dusk. The light from the setting sun silhouetted the yacht's sleek shape, its sails furled against the backdrop of deep blue waters and emerald green islets. Golden shafts of light painted everything in unbelievably vivid hues, as though framing the whole picture for eternity.

Silently the crew rolled out deep red carpets on the freshly scrubbed deck, and then the master emerged in his crisp white "tropics" to survey the situation. By now there were canoes all around as curious islanders wanted to be a part of this experience, this change.

Our members were caught up in the excitement. They soon brought back reports, and even though I was young and inexperienced, it did not take long to realize what was happening.

The man was a millionaire from overseas, cruising the world. He wanted to trade for food and water, and he wanted girls. There was liquor on board and a real "swinging time" for those who would accept his invitation.

I counseled the members to stay away. Most did, but some did not. The wealthy adventurer stayed for a few days until he filled his wants. Then he announced he would leave before noon the following day. Some of the faithful members pleaded, "Can we go out before he leaves, just to see the boat?" I agreed that at ten o'clock the next morning we would briefly look at the yacht.

When we got there, it was even more elegant than I had pictured. Evidence of the previous night's activities was still being cleared away, and preparations were being made to raise anchor and take sail. We spent a few moments in wonder and awe, astonished at the beauty of the deep mahogany paneling, the rich bronze fittings, the luster of the freshly painted surfaces, and the gleaming white of the hull as it lapped quietly at the deep blue lagoon.

We got in our canoes. The owner, nearly sober, waved good-bye, and we returned to shore. As we pulled our dugouts onto the sandy beach, I turned again to see that sleek, white form move toward the horizon. I thought of the millionaire in his white "tropics," having had his fill, comfortable with his well-stocked cupboards and expert crew, with his money and power. He seemed to have everything he wanted.

Then I looked at the men who had brought me to shore: no shoes, shirts of rags, tattered *valas* (skirts) tied with coconut sennit around their waists. I looked past them to the village. I saw the smoke from the morning's cooking twisting lazily into the air, heard the monotonous sound of *tapa* being beaten, and felt the heaviness of the overhead sun as it filtered through the palm trees. I watched the men slowly walk to their gardens and heard the laughter of naked children as they chased scrawny dogs.

Suddenly the oppressiveness of island life, with so little opportunity for change, struck me as being grossly unfair. I turned again to gaze at the yacht, now receding into the distance. The contrast was so great as to be almost unbelievable. My heart cried out, "Unfair! Unfair! These poor people—look at them. And you—look at you!"

I returned to the group, and we trudged up the shore to the village. Then one of the older men turned to me and said softly in his native tongue, "I am very sad. I feel very sorry."

"Well," I interrupted, "I am very sad, and I feel very sorry, too. It just isn't fair, is it?"

"No," he continued, "it really isn't fair. I feel so sorry for him, for he will never be happy."

I stopped dead in my tracks.

"*You* feel sorry for *him? He* won't be happy? What are you talking about?"

My mind was groping to come to an understanding of what he had just said. This man with nothing was saying he was sorry for that man with everything! My immature mind was spinning, trying to interpret words, feelings, and relationships.

The islander continued: "I feel sorry for him. He will never be happy, for he seeks only his own pleasure, not to help others. Yet we know that happiness comes from helping others. All he will do is sail around the world seeking happiness, hoping others will bring it to him, but they cannot. He will never find it, for he has not learned to help others. He has too much money, too many luxuries, too much power. Oh, I feel so sorry for him."

I looked at the wrinkled brown body of the old man. His teeth were gone, his hair was white, and his skin was leather. But his eyes were soft, his voice quiet, and his countenance immaculate. His powerful words had taught me a great lesson.

Years have passed, but occasionally as I see proud people traveling in their sleek, new cars or sense my own unwillingness to help others, I close my eyes and see a beautiful yacht moving toward the horizon, then see an old man with a wrinkled, brown body, white hair, and skin of leather. I listen as his soft eyes penetrate mine. His toothless mouth moves and his spirit explains: "I feel sorry for him. He will never be happy. He hasn't learned to help others."

"Thank You for the Fleas"

CORRIE TEN BOOM

Editor's Note: Dutch sisters Corrie and Betsie ten Boom were sent to a concentration camp for assisting Jews during the Nazis' onslaught in Holland. Both sisters, well into their fifties when they arrived in Ravensbruck, learned invaluable lessons in that horrible death camp. The following is an example of their ability to find happiness and gratitude for blessings amidst such terrible oppression.

The move to permanent quarters came the second week in October. We were marched, ten abreast, along a wide cinder avenue and then into a narrower street of barracks. Several times the column halted while numbers were read out—names were never used at Ravensbruck. At last Betsie's and mine were called: "Prisoner 66729, Prisoner 66730." We stepped out of line with a dozen or so others and stared at the long gray front of Barracks 28. Half its windows seemed to have been broken and replaced with rags. A door in the center let us into a large room where two hundred or more women bent over knitting needles. On tables between them were piles of woolen socks in army gray.

On either side doors opened into two still larger rooms—by far the largest dormitories we had yet seen. Betsie and I followed a prisoner-guide through the door at the right. Because of the broken windows the vast room was in semi-twilight. Our noses told us, first, that the place was filthy: somewhere plumbing had backed up, the bedding was soiled and rancid. Then as our eyes adjusted to the gloom we saw that there were no individual beds at all, but great square piers stacked three high, and wedged side by side and end to end with only an occasional narrow aisle slicing through.

We followed our guide single file—the aisle was not wide enough for two—fighting back the claustrophobia of these platforms rising everywhere above us. The tremendous room was nearly empty of people; they must have been out on various work crews. At last she pointed to a second tier in the center of a large block. To reach it we had to stand on the bottom level, haul ourselves up, and then crawl across three other straw-covered platforms to reach the one that we would share with—how many? The deck above us was too close to let us sit up. We lay back, struggling against the nausea that swept over us from the reeking straw. We could hear the women who had arrived with us finding their places.

Suddenly I sat up, striking my head on the cross-slats above. Something had pinched my leg.

"Fleas!" I cried. "Betsie, the place is swarming with them!"

We scrambled across the intervening platforms, heads low to avoid another bump, dropped down to the aisle, and edged our way to a patch of light.

"Here! And here another one!" I wailed. "Betsie, how can we live in such a place!"

"Show us. Show us how." It was said so matter of factly it took me a second to realize she was praying. More and more the distinction between prayer and the rest of life seemed to be vanishing for Betsie.

"Corrie!" she said excitedly. "He's given us the answer! Before we asked, as He always does! In the Bible this morning. Where was it? Read that part again!"

I glanced down the long dim aisle to make sure no guard was in sight, then drew the Bible from its pouch. "It was in First Thessalonians," I said. We were on our third complete reading of the New Testament since leaving Scheveningen. In the feeble light I turned the pages. "Here it is: 'Comfort the frightened, help the weak, be patient with everyone. See that none of you repays evil for evil, but always seek to do good to one another and to all. . . .'" It seemed written expressly to Ravensbruck.

"Go on," said Betsie. "That wasn't all."

"Oh yes: '. . . to one another and to all. Rejoice always, pray constantly, give thanks in all circumstances; for this is the will of God in Christ Jesus—"

"That's it, Corrie! That's His answer. 'Give thanks in all circumstances!' That's what we can do. We can start right now to thank God for every single thing about this new barracks!"

I stared at her, then around me at the dark, foul-aired room. "Such as?" I said.

"Such as being assigned here together."

I bit my lip. "Oh yes, Lord Jesus!"

"Such as what you're holding in your hands."

I looked down at the Bible. "Yes! Thank You, dear Lord, that there was no inspection when we entered here! Thank You for all the women, here in this room, who will meet You in these pages."

"Yes," said Betsie. "Thank You for the very crowding here. Since we're packed so close, that many more will hear!" She looked at me expectantly. "Corrie!" she prodded.

"Oh, all right. Thank You for the jammed, crammed, stuffed, packed, suffocating crowds."

"Thank You," Betsie went on serenely, "for the fleas and for—"

The fleas! This was too much. "Betsie, there's no way even God can make me grateful for a flea."

" 'Give thanks in *all* circumstances,' " she quoted. "It doesn't say, 'in pleasant circumstances.' Fleas are part of this place where God has put us."

And so we stood between piers of bunks and gave thanks for fleas. But this time I was sure Betsie was wrong.

One evening I got back to the barracks late from a wood-gathering foray outside the walls. A light snow lay on the ground and it was hard to find the sticks and twigs with which a small stove was kept going in each room. Betsie was waiting for me, as always, so that we could wait through the food line together. Her eyes were twinkling.

"You're looking extraordinarily pleased with yourself," I told her.

"You know we've never understood why we had so much freedom in the big room," she said. "Well—I've found out."

That afternoon, she said, there'd been confusion in her knitting group about sock sizes and they'd asked the supervisor to come and settle it.

"But she wouldn't. She wouldn't step through the door and neither would the guards. And you know why?"

Betsie could not keep the triumph from her voice: "Because of the fleas! That's what she said, 'That place is crawling with fleas!'"

My mind rushed back to our first hour in this place. I remembered Betsie's bowed head, remembered her thanks to God for creatures I could see no use for.

My Little Bread and Butter Life

Catherine B. Pratt

Apr. 12, 05

I love my bread and butter life
Nor would I change it for another.
I'm just an average sort of wife,
An ordinary sort of mother.
I feel that fancy things are vain
Like caviar on gold-trimmed dishes,
Contentedly, I find my plain
Old bread and butter is delicious.
For me there's no monotony
Because of one-meal repetition,
And I look forward gratefully
To each meal's pleasure and nutrition.
I know that others yearn for more
And find my bread and butter meager;
But, often, all they're looking for
Leaves them somewhat more bored than eager,
And I have friends that I love dearly,
Whose lives are bread and butter, too.
We share our simple tastes and clearly
Old-hat, old-fashioned point of view.
So let those who desire their pheasant
With its accompanying strife,
Have all they want. What I find pleasant?
My little bread and butter life!

*D*ad's Gratitude

H. DAVID BURTON

Heavenly Father knew that *this* strong-willed son needed a good father. He picked out a great one for me. My dad's devotion to his children and grandchildren consumed much of his time. He loved the Lord and was about the Lord's errand throughout his days. He was not only my dad; he was one of my heroes.

Dad was the president of my priests quorum and bishop of our ward during my teenage years. You who have been a bishop's son know that sometimes performance expectations tend to be a little high for bishops' sons.

During Dad's tenure as bishop, a new meetinghouse was built in our area. Local financial shares were partially fulfilled by providing labor. Often I arrived home to find a note on the kitchen table inviting me to join Dad in working on the new building. These invitations were not always received with great warmth and enthusiasm. It seemed to me the bishop's son received more than his fair share of invitations to work on the new meetinghouse.

As the building neared completion, landscaping commenced. The priesthood brethren were extended a work opportunity in hauling fertilizer to the site. Because the bishop was a part of the expedition, the bishop's son felt an obligation to respond. We drove to a mountain sheep corral. Into a large truck we shoveled very finely ground, dry, sheep fertilizer. The wind blew much of what we threw into the truck back to us. This unsavory material gathered in our eyes, our throats, our noses, ears, and down our backs. I can't ever remember being more uncomfortable. I'm afraid I verbalized my feelings with emotion. When we arrived back at the meetinghouse to unload the material, I found my new bike had been *stolen*. My complaining was loud. Why would the Lord permit someone to steal my bike when I was about His work?

When Dad and I arrived home, we showered and sat down to an evening meal. My complaining about the day and my lost bike continued. As we knelt in prayer, Dad thanked Heavenly Father for the opportunity of the day's service and expressed love for me. He asked forgiveness for the person who had taken the bike. He noted his sorrow for the loss but expressed gratitude that it wasn't his son who had committed the theft.

Eliza Roxcy Snow and Seeing the "Better Side"

GARRETT H. GARFF

Drip. *Drop. Drip. Drop.* Inside the little log hut, forty-four-year-old Eliza Roxcy Snow watched the water drops fall from the roof. Made from dirt and willows, the practically flat roof could not keep out the steady rain. So much for what some had said about the Salt Lake Valley not getting a lot of rain!

It was March of 1848. Eliza had arrived in the Valley with a company of Latter-day Saints the previous fall and had spent the winter in this small one-room dwelling.

She was no stranger to bad living conditions and other hardships. During the thirteen-hundred-mile journey from Nauvoo, Illinois, to the Salt Lake Valley she had faced many challenges. She had been exposed to the cold and wet weather. She had known what it was like to be bone-tired. She had experienced the dangers of prairie fires and cattle stampedes. And at times she had been sick; in fact, on one occasion she had been so sick that she nearly died.

Yet it was not Eliza's way to complain or to get discouraged. Instead, she found ways to help others not get discouraged. Often she did this through her poetry. She loved to write. (One time when she was literally down to her last dime, she used it to buy a bottle of ink for writing.) But what pleased her most was being able to use her talents in the service of her brothers and sisters in the Church.

So it was that during the trek she wrote a poem to help cheer up a friend. In that poem Eliza showed that not only did she have the vision of a poet, but more important, she had the vision of one in tune with the Spirit.

> Thou much belov'd in Zion!
>   Remember life is made
> A double-sided picture,
>   Contrasting light and shade.
>
> Our Father means to prove us—
>   And here we're fully tried.
> He will reverse the drawing
>   And show the *better* side.

Through her devotion to the Lord and his gospel, Eliza was often allowed to see the "better side" of whatever circumstance she was in.

But now, here in this hut with the leaky roof, she might have wondered if there could possibly be a "better side" to her situation.

It was bedtime, and so as more and more drops of water came through the roof, Eliza got into her bed, opened an umbrella, and spread it over her head and shoulders. At least part of her would remain dry!

Before long the *drip-drop* of the rain was joined by a new sound: *clink, clink, clink.* It took Eliza only a moment to realize what it was. Some of the rocks that were mixed in with the dirt roof were now dropping down to the floor.

But that was not all. From various parts of the hut came a high-pitched noise: *squeak, squeak, squeak.* Mice were scurrying about, trying to find a place to get away from the rain.

The little log hut was a symphony of sound!

Eliza looked down at the lower part of her bed, which, because it was not covered by the umbrella, was getting wetter by the minute. By morning she would probably look as if she had been wading through a river.

And then she just couldn't help herself. Eliza began to laugh. How could she not? The whole scene was just so ridiculous!

Once again, Eliza Roxcy Snow had seen the "better side." In doing so, she proved the truth of one of her own observations: "None but Saints can be happy under every circumstance."

"*I* Can Feel Just as Well as Anybody"

GEORGE ALBERT SMITH

A Holland brother by the name of Folkers was living with his wife at my place, and they could not speak or understand the English language. He used to go to the fast meetings, and when the other people talked, he could not understand what they said. When they finished, he would get up and talk, and we could not understand him. One day I asked him, "Why do you go to the English-speaking services? You cannot understand." It took me sometime to make him understand what I wanted to know. Finally he smiled and said: "It is not what you hear that makes you happy; nor what you see that makes you happy; it is what you feel, and I can feel just as well as anybody."

*M*iguel Had No Shoes

ALLAN K. BURGESS AND MAX H. MOLGARD

The vital attitudes of humility and gratitude were illustrated well by a young father, Miguel, who lived in the mountains of Guatemala. He was poor in terms of worldly possessions, but rich in testimony and faith. His shirt was ragged, his pants held together with more patches than original material, and he owned no shoes. He had received little formal education, could not read or write, and he made less than three hundred dollars a year.

Miguel served as a counselor in the small Church branch in his area. The branch met in a bamboo hut that was deteriorating rapidly. The roof sagged just a little bit more each week, stark evidence that the hut would not last much longer.

The missionaries in the area were teaching a young couple who were preparing for marriage, and they were overjoyed when the couple desired to be baptized. They planned to be married and baptized the same day.

On the selected day, the couple made the long bus trip to a neighboring city. The missionaries accompanied the couple and invited Miguel to travel with them. However, the marriage and baptism took longer than expected, so the return bus had already left. They could get a ride back to the main road, but that left them with a challenging walk of seventeen miles back to the area where they lived. Because of a serious gas shortage, they knew that there was little chance of a car driving by that would give them a ride.

The couple had some relatives in the city, so they could stay. But Miguel needed to get home so he could go to work the next morning. He and the missionaries set out to walk the seventeen miles. After walking for many hours, they came to the steep two-mile climb that would finally bring them home.

One of the missionaries was murmuring to himself, asking God why they had to go through this physical torture. Then he glanced over at Miguel and saw a big smile on his face. This missionary could not think of anything to smile about after fifteen miles of walking, so he asked Miguel why he was so happy. Miguel's response taught him a great lesson, for he said, "I am so happy because we just witnessed two people become members of God's true Church." The missionary looked down at Miguel's bare feet, thought of the smile that had lasted for fifteen miles, and, through Miguel, came to realize how wonderful it was to introduce the gospel to others. His fatigue and anger were replaced with gratitude and humility for the opportunity they had received of teaching and baptizing a wonderful couple.

Just a few weeks later, the devotion of Miguel was illustrated even further. The bamboo chapel had deteriorated to the point that the last meeting was being held there. During the meeting, Miguel stood up and announced that he had been secretly building another chapel for the branch and that it was completed and ready to meet in. Miguel had to work twelve hours a day, six days a week, just to earn a meager living for his family; yet he had taken nearly every penny he made and all of his extra time during the previous six months to prepare a special meeting place. He still didn't have any shoes, but he had appreciated the gospel and the members so much that he had wanted to do something special for them and for the Lord. Because of his tremendous faith and dedication, the Lord had blessed him so that the needs of his family had been taken care of.

$\mathscr{A}$ Poor Memory

Richard M. Siddoway

$\mathbf{G}$reat wisdom is often delivered in small doses. When I was fourteen years of age my family moved to a new house—at least, it was new to us. The first Sunday I attended church I met other young men of the ward who took me into their circle of friendship and who, today, I view as lifelong friends.

"Do you like basketball?" I was asked as we walked home from school the following Friday afternoon.

"Sure. I like it, but I'm not very good at it," I replied honestly.

"That doesn't matter. We're going up to the church in the morning. Want to come along?"

In the ward I had moved from there were very tight rules about using the church gymnasium. You had to have an adult present, and you had to schedule the time you wanted to use it at least a week in advance. Most of us felt it wasn't worth the effort. Some of the older boys learned how to stick small pebbles against the doorjamb so that the door wouldn't close tightly, and then they'd come back to play unannounced and certainly unwelcomed. Our church custodian, who oversaw the use of the building, seemed to glory in his power. If and when he caught any unauthorized visitors, it generally meant a visit with the bishop, the parents, and the offenders.

"Did you schedule the building?" I asked with my previous experiences in mind. "Who's coming with us?"

"Oh, just a bunch of the guys are going up to play a little ball. Brother Percy won't mind."

"Who is Brother Percy?" I queried.

"He's the custodian. His real name is Percival—Percival Roberts. He's real cool."

"And he'll just let us in?" I couldn't believe my ears.

"Oh, he'll probably be there cleaning anyway. He never seems to stop cleaning. But if he isn't, he lives in the house next to the church, and he'll let us in or give us a key."

This was unbelievable to me, but the next morning when we arrived at the church, the doors were open. "Brother Percy?" Dale, my next-door neighbor, called out, "Okay if we play a little ball?"

Immediately a little gnome of a man popped out of a classroom. "Sure, me boys. Just remember where you are." Percival Roberts stared at the group of us. "And who's the new chap?" he asked, nodding his head in my direction. He fairly skipped down the hall and grabbed my hand. "I'm Percival Roberts," he said, shaking my hand vigorously, "though most just call me Percy. And who might you be?"

At fourteen years of age—a small fourteen years of age—I looked Brother Roberts square in the eye. His head was covered with a carefully combed thatch of pure white hair. His bright blue eyes twinkled above rosy cheeks. A pair of wire-rimmed spectacles perched on his button nose. And a broad, broad smile covered his face. He was wearing a pair of ancient striped coveralls over what appeared to be red long johns.

I introduced myself while he continued to look in my eyes and pump my hand. "Glad to have you aboard," he said in his broad British accent. "Boys," he said, almost apologetically, "I've got to have you out of here by noon. We've got a ward dinner in here this evening, and the high priests are coming to set up tables at twelve." He nodded toward Dale, who was carrying the basketball. "Now, give me a shot." Dale bounced the basketball toward Brother Percy, who tilted his head and launched the ball toward the basket from the doorway of the gymnasium. The ball fell five feet short of the basket. "I'm getting closer," he laughed as he spun around and whisked down the hallway toward the classroom he'd been cleaning.

We played a spirited game of basketball for the next two hours. No one kept score; we just had fun. Suddenly Brother Percy popped into the gym. "Have to sweep the floor now, me boy-ohs. Whew! And we might want to air the place out a bit."

He waved his hand in front of his nose. "But give me one more shot." I bounced the ball to him. He eyed the basket and tried a two-handed set shot from the foul line. This time he actually hit the back-board. "I'm getting better," he chortled.

"Want some help?" Dale asked.

"I never turn down an offer like that. You know what they say—many hands make light work." And Brother Percy handed an enormous dust mop to Dale. In fifteen minutes we had swept the floor and helped Brother Percy set up folding tables and chairs for the ward dinner.

"I thought you said the high priests were coming over to do this," I said.

"They're busy men," said Brother Percy, "and just think what a surprise we have for them when they get here! Thank you for your help."

I never knew whether any high priests showed up, or whether any were supposed to show up. I just knew that things were going to be ready for a ward dinner that night. "He's real nice," I exclaimed later to Dale.

"Yeah, Brother Percy's great. Not much of a basketball player, though. He takes a shot or two every time we're there, and I've never seen him make a basket."

"Does he take care of the building all by himself?" I asked.

Dale's face darkened. "Almost. His wife helps him. Boy, is she different from Brother Percy." There were nods of agreement among the rest of my newfound friends. "If she's there . . . well, sometimes it's just easier to go home."

"How come?"

"Well, she gives us a hard time for being there, and she gives Brother Percy a hard time for letting us in. She's just always . . ." He struggled for the right word. "She's sort of . . . well, you'll meet her soon enough.

Dale was right. The next morning at church, Brother Percy was sitting by the door to the chapel as we entered. He jumped to his feet and extended his hand. "Welcome, me boy-oh, these beautiful people must be the rest of your family. I'm Brother Roberts," he said, shaking each of my family's hands. "And this lovely woman is my wife, Gwynith." He gestured toward the woman who had been sitting, and was still sitting, on the bench next to him. My father extended his hand toward her. She reluctantly took it as if examining a rather unpleasant specimen. She smiled a thin, brittle smile with lips pressed together so hard they left a white ring around her mouth, and inclined her head in the tiniest of nods. My mother's proffered hand received similar treatment. Mine was left dangling in front of her. She merely expelled a quiet huff and turned her head away from me. After an uncomfortable moment I retrieved my hand and found a seat.

The following Saturday a half dozen of us arrived at the chapel for another game of basketball. Brother Percy bobbed out of a classroom as he heard the door open. "Can we play a little ball, Brother Percy?"

He fairly skipped down the hallway toward the gymnasium. "Only if I get me shot, boy-ohs." He took the proffered basketball and launched it toward the basket. "Another air ball," he said as the ball fell short of the basket. "Ah, well, that leaves me room for improvement. Have fun." He turned and flew down the hallway.

Half an hour later we were sweating profusely, and took a break to get a drink from the fountain in the hall. As I bent over the gleaming stainless steel fountain, I heard the door open behind me.

"Who in the world let you foul urchins in here?" Sister Roberts screamed.

"Uh-oh," said Dale under his breath.

"Why do I even try?" she exploded as she cast her eyes upward at the ceiling and shook her hands above her head. "It isn't enough I work my fingers to the bone cleaning this building every day. Now I have to put up with you smelly little beggars fouling the air the day before the Sabbath." At that moment Brother Percy popped out of a room down the hallway.

"Ah, Gwynith, my sweet. What brings you here today? The boys were just having a friendly game of basketball. No harm done."

"Percival Walkingham Roberts!" she screeched "I thought

we had an understanding. You know the rules as well as I. These boys are not to be here unsupervised. You never know what mischief they'll get into." She shook her finger in Brother Robert's face.

"Ah, my sweet, they're good chaps. They don't give me any grief, and they often help with me chores." He shrugged his shoulders and his lips formed a half smile.

"We were just going," interjected Dale. "Hope we didn't upset anything." We fairly flew out the door.

"They're sure different," I mused as we walked home. "He's so nice, and she's so . . ."

"Well, my mom says opposites attract," replied Dale.

The next morning at church, Brother and Sister Roberts were again sitting by the back door of the chapel. Apparently it was their usual spot. "Good morning," Brother Roberts beamed as he leapt to his feet and shook hands with my family. Sister Roberts remained seated with her white-rimmed lips.

"I'm sorry if we caused problems yesterday," I began. Brother Roberts shook his head. His wife sniffed and turned her head away from me.

"No problem, me boy-oh, you're always welcome in the Lord's house."

Sister Roberts's head snapped back as she glared at her husband. The white rim around her lips grew more pronounced. Then, with a shudder, she looked straight ahead toward the pulpit.

Our basketball games continued into the winter months. Brother Percy always greeted us as if we were long-lost friends. He'd take the basketball and try a shot or two, never making a basket; then leave us to play. If his wife appeared, we disappeared.

One Saturday night it began to snow. Dale called me on the telephone just as I was getting ready for bed. "We're going to go help shovel snow around the church early tomorrow morning. Want to come?"

"Sure," I said. "What time?"

"Well, the first meeting's at eight-thirty, so we're going up about seven o'clock."

"I'll be ready."

By seven o'clock there were about ten inches of snow on the ground. Dale and I arrived at the church and found the walks were already shoveled. Brother Percy was just finishing the last sidewalk to the back door when we showed up. "Ah, me boy-ohs, you've come to help, have you? Well, we've got this wee bit of snow to get off the path before the people start arriving. Thrust in your shovels and we'll have it done in a jiffy."

Within five minutes the last bit of snow had been removed. "How early did you have to get up to do this?" I asked.

"I'm an early riser, me boy-ohs. I started shoveling about five o'clock. But I do appreciate your help. I think I'm getting a little older, if not wiser." He chuckled as he waved a mittened hand to us and started next door toward home.

Later that morning as we entered church, Brother Roberts jumped to his feet from his seat near the door. As he pumped my hand he said, "It was a real help, it was, to have you boys help with the snow shoveling this morning."

"Humph," snorted Sister Roberts. "The old fool's going to die from the cold one of these days," she exclaimed to no one in particular.

The winter snows melted and the rebirth of spring brought new challenges to our chapel. Flowers had to be planted and weeds pulled. The trees needed to be pruned, the grass mowed and edged. Brother Roberts was everywhere, it seemed. "You sure work hard," I said one day as we helped plant petunias in the flower beds.

"Ah, it wouldn't be right to have someone think ill of the Lord's house just because old Percy's too lazy to keep it clean, now, would it?" He smiled. "And I do appreciate you boys helping. I know you're busy, too." It seemed like scant payment for the use of the gymnasium all year long. "Besides, who knows when you won't be able to make your little contribution?"

One Sunday late in June, the bishop was conducting sacrament meeting. "I have a few announcements to make," he began. "The annual Fourth of July breakfast will be held in the parking lot behind the church at seven A.M. We will have a flag raising by the Scout troop followed by breakfast. Remember to bring your own plates and utensils." He paused. "This next announcement is a hard one for me to make. I've grown to love Brother Roberts so much . . . and Sister Roberts. He's taken such loving care of this building. But he's decided it's time to retire. Brother and Sister Roberts are going to travel back to their native England on a well-deserved vacation next month. We're going to have a little reception to honor them next Saturday evening. We hope all of you can attend. The reception will be from seven until nine o'clock. There will be light refreshments served."

The entire congregation from both wards that used our building attended the reception. People who had moved away years before returned to wish the Robertses well. The obligatory punch and cookies were served throughout the evening.

Finally the bishop stood and asked Brother and Sister Roberts to come to the stand. "Brother Percy," said the bishop, "you have been a faithful servant of the Lord and of the people of these two wards. You and your wife have made this building the pride of the neighborhood. I'm sure this little remembrance is insufficient to pay you for your tireless efforts over the past twenty-three years, but we'd like to give it to you anyway and hear a word or two from you and your wife." He handed Brother Roberts a gift wrapped in silver paper. Brother Roberts handed it to his wife and whispered something in her ear.

Sister Roberts pursed her lips tightly. She walked to the microphone. The bishop adjusted the microphone stand and lowered the microphone a foot to her height.

"You'll never know the work that's gone into this building," she began. "You've paid Percy for forty hours each week, and he's given at least sixty. He's never taken a vacation in twenty-three years." Her voice was rising in pitch and volume. "I've tried to make the old fool see that he wasn't being paid enough. But he just wouldn't listen. Well, he may be sorry to be leaving this job, but I'm not. I've had to put up with no time off just as he has." She lifted the glittering silver package in her hands. "No sorry little gift is going to make up for the sacrifice we've had to make. I'm sure this isn't what you wanted to hear, but I felt it needed to be said." She walked back to her seat. Total silence enveloped the hall.

Percival Roberts walked to the microphone. It did not have to be adjusted for his height. He ran his fingers through his snow-white thatch. "My dear brothers and sisters," he began. "It has been my privilege for nearly a quarter of a century to help in some small way with this beautiful building. Every Sunday you good people have come here to worship the Lord. I have seen babies blessed, children baptized and confirmed, wedding receptions, and funerals. It has been my pleasure to help prepare a place for those events . . . some filled with joy, some with sorrow. During these years I have had the help of some of the best people in this world. Many of you have helped clean this building, plant flowers, and shovel snow. This service will not go unnoticed, I am sure. I have had the blessing of associating with eight different bishops during my tour of duty. Each of them has been a special, dedicated man. None of them has been perfect, but then, neither am I. If I have been able to make your worship a little easier through any of my poor efforts, then my reward has already been felt. The young men and women who come to play basketball and volleyball are such great young people. They have treated me with such kindness. I cannot remember when a single act of vandalism has happened to this building. Those who were young when we began our labors have grown older. Many have married and begun families of their own. A few have moved back into this very neighborhood.

"Now, none of this could have happened without the help of all of you. But especially I could not have contributed my small piece without the total support of my dear wife, Gwynith."

A murmur went through the crowd, then all was quiet again. "My sweet Gwynith and I have been married for forty-one years.

You know, brothers and sisters, I have been blessed so abundantly. One of those great blessings is Gwynith." He paused a moment and removed his spectacles. "I cannot remember once in that forty-one years when Gwynith has ever uttered an unkind word."

The entire congregation stared in disbelief.

"Another of those great blessings is . . . a poor memory."

Sometimes great wisdom is delivered in small doses.

Service
and
Sacrifice

Lord, Make Me an Instrument of Your Peace

ST. FRANCIS OF ASSISI

Lord,
make me an instrument of Your peace.
Where there is hatred let me sow love;
Where there is injury, pardon;
Where there is doubt, faith;
Where there is despair, hope;
Where there is darkness, light; and
Where there is sadness, joy.
O divine Master,
grant that I may not so much
Seek to be consoled as to console;
To be understood as to understand;
To be loved as to love;
For it is in giving that we receive;
It is in pardoning that we are pardoned; and
It is in dying that we are born to eternal life.

You Never Know Who
You May Save

JACOB DE JAGER

I would like to go back in thought to my native Holland where six generations of my father's ancestors lived in the little village of Scheveningen at the seashore. They were fishermen or had other related vocations, like fishing-boat builders, sailmakers, or fishing-net repairmen. Many of them were also involved in the voluntary but hazardous task of lifesaving. They were stouthearted, experienced men who always were ready to man the rowing lifeboats to go on a rescue mission. With every westerly gale that blew, some fishing boats ran into difficulties, and many times the sailors had to cling to the rigging of their stricken ships in a desperate fight to escape inevitable drowning. Year after year the sea claimed its victims.

On one occasion during a severe storm, a ship was in distress, and a rowboat went out to rescue the crew of the fishing boat. The waves were enormous, and each of the men at the oars had to give all his strength and energy to reach the unfortunate sailors in the grim darkness of the night and the heavy rainstorm.

The trip to the wrecked ship was successful, but the rowboat was too small to take the whole crew in one rescue operation. One man had to stay behind on board because there simply was no room for him; the risk that the rescue boat would capsize was too great. When the rescuers made it back to the beach, hundreds of people were waiting for them with torches to guide them in the dreary night. But the same crew could not make the second trip because they were exhausted from their fight with the stormwinds, the waves, and the sweeping rains.

So the local captain of the coast guard asked for volunteers to make a second trip. Among those who stepped forward without hesitation was a nineteen-year-old youth by the name of Hans. With his mother he had come to the beach in his oil-skin clothes to watch the rescue operation.

When Hans stepped forward his mother panicked and said, "Hans, please don't go. Your father died at sea when you were four years old and your older brother Pete has been reported missing at sea for more than three months now. You are the only son left to me!"

But Hans said, "Mom, I feel I have to do it. It is my duty." And the mother wept and restlessly started pacing the beach when Hans boarded the rowing boat, took the oars, and disappeared into the night.

After a struggle with the high-going seas that lasted for more than an hour (and to Hans's mother it seemed an eternity), the rowboat came into sight again. When the rescuers had approached the beach close enough so that the captain of the coast guard could reach them by shouting, he cupped his hands around his mouth and called vigorously against the storm, "Did you save him?"

And then the people lighting the sea with their torches saw Hans rise from his rowing bench, and he shouted with all his might. "Yes! And tell Mother it is my brother Pete!"

Gospel Givers

Leland E. Anderson

I am indebted to President A. Theodore Tuttle of the First Council of the Seventy for the following story.

While he was teaching seminary in Brigham City, Utah, he said, he knew a wonderful bishop who owned many acres of land in the western part of the county. One year he was blessed with an exceptionally large crop. He had sold thousands of bushels of hard wheat. When he went out to get the last load from the threshing, with his big truck carrying about ten tons, he wondered what he would do with it. He had a big bank account, all his silos were filled with wheat, and thousands of bushels had been sold. He thought a while, then said, "I know what I'll do—I'll give it to Brother John."

Brother John, who lived in this bishop's ward, had just been married. He and his wife had built a large chicken coop and were raising white leghorn chickens so they would have eggs to sell.

The bishop felt that nothing would be better than to give this young couple a boost in life. I'm not unmindful of the rich man in the New Testament who had a similar experience, except that his experience ended terribly. When he looked at his crops and all his barns loaded, he said to himself, "What will I do with all this increase? I know what I will do; I will tear my barns down and will build bigger ones. I will load them with the fruits of my labors." This man had forgotten to distinguish between what was the Lord's and what was his.

So the bishop drove up to the home of Brother John, backed his truck into the lot, and went up and knocked on the door. When he found there was no one home, he said, "Thank the Lord." Then he backed up against the big empty silo and put the machinery to work, and it wasn't long until he had the silo nearly filled with wheat. Then he drove off.

Two or three weeks passed. One day he met the young man on the sidewalk downtown. Brother John said to him, "Bishop, I have a problem. Someone by mistake has emptied a load of wheat and filled my silo. Now my chickens got into some of it this morning, and they sure like it, but I'm sure some farmer had a helper who didn't know where to unload it and put it in my granary by mistake. I'm wondering, inasmuch as you're a farmer, if you know anyone else who's been hauling grain into town."

With a twinkle in his eye, the bishop responded: "Brother John, if I were you, I would never try to find out who that man was."

Then Brother John realized the answer. He grabbed the bishop by the hand and said, "God bless you, dear Bishop. I think I knew all the time who had done that work." The young man whipped out his checkbook, opened it, got out a pen, and started to write out a check. "How much do I owe you for that wheat?" he asked.

The bishop said, "John, put that checkbook back in your pocket. And as long as you live, don't think you owe me anything. If you live to be a million years old, you could not pay me for that wheat."

So both of them went on their way, rejoicing in the commandment of the Lord to love your neighbor as yourself.

A couple of weeks later was Thanksgiving, and the bishop went down to the meat locker to get some choice meat for Thanksgiving dinner. As he opened the door, he saw that the locker was filled with dressed chickens. He smiled, took what he needed, and went on his way with a lighter step.

A week later he met John on the street and said, "John, I have a problem. Someone by mistake has put a lot of dressed chickens in one of my meat lockers. And since you're in the chicken business, I thought you might know who's been killing chickens around town, because I want to pay for them."

John replied, "Bishop, if I were you I would never try to find out." At that, the bishop pulled out of his pocketbook a roll of bills and started to peel off some of the big ones. But John said, "You put that money back in your pocket. If you live to be a million years old, you couldn't pay me for those chickens."

This is the true spirit of the gospel of Jesus Christ.

Nadine's Dance

GRANT H. TAYLOR

Ed and Stacey were student-body officers in the high school where I once taught. Ed was an honor student and very capable in anything he tried. Even though not a real jock, he was a tennis star and very well liked by everyone he met. Stacey was the type of girl that every teenage girl dreams of being—cute, sparkly, witty, able to say just the right thing at the right time, popular with everyone—and she was very interested in Ed.

Nadine was not one of my students. She took mostly special-education classes. She was slow of speech and walked awkwardly and with a slight limp. She made every effort to be friendly with everyone, but with all that she gave, you still saw Nadine alone by her locker most of the time. She came into my room often that year because I worked with the student-body officers and she found in them a group who showed her acceptance and friendship. It was obvious that she was crying out for compassion, starving for a little affection. She found it, to some degree, with these student-body officers, and so she began skipping her own classes to come in and just sit in the room with them. Ed, especially, went out of his way to be kind to her.

Two weeks prior to the big girls' preference dance, Ed was

in Washington, D.C., on one of many trips he earned through his scholastic excellence. Stacey came to me for suggestions on how she might concoct a truly unique, never-tried-before way of asking Ed to go with her to the dance. It was decided that she would send a telegram to the hotel in Washington where he was staying. This she did. The telegram arrived. Ed was duly impressed. Upon his arrival home he accepted Stacey's invitation in an equally creative way, and they made plans: dress color, tux style, restaurant reservations—the works.

Then, just four days before the dance, Nadine approached Ed in the hall and asked him to be her partner at the girls' pref dance.

Now, Ed had every right and every legal reason in the world to respectfully turn her down. He could explain to her that he had already accepted an invitation and that plans had been made and finalized. He really had no obligation to do otherwise—except for one thing: Ed knew Nadine and he knew her background. He knew that she had never been to any kind of dance with anyone. He knew how most boys would turn her down without even thinking. But he also knew he had accepted Stacey's invitation and that she had made a new dress, had planned a very special evening, and had counted on this date for several weeks.

So he told Nadine that he thought he had to work that night but would see if he could get it off and would get back to her. Then he went to Stacey and told her the situation.

Stacey was not only pretty, bright, and popular; she was someone who was acquainted with her Father in Heaven—and so was Ed. (Thank heaven that there are kids like those two in the world!) Stacey did a most admirable thing and made it possible for Ed to do an even more admirable thing. She said, "You take Nadine to the dance. I will have many more opportunities. This may be the only one Nadine will have in her entire life."

Ed took Nadine to the dance. It was hard for him. It was the most glorious evening in Nadine's life to that point. I know because I talked to her the next day. Stacey stayed home, with her new dress hanging in the closet. To this day Stacey and Ed are not sorry for the good thing that they did.

Someone to Do For

BOYD K. PACKER

Shortly after the funeral held for the first wife of President Harold B. Lee, I was in a group which included his daughter Helen. Someone expressed sympathy to her for the passing of her mother and said: "She took such good care of your father. I'm sure he must be lonely and must miss all of the things she did for him."

Helen responded with an insight of remarkable wisdom. "You do not understand," she said. "It is not so much that he misses all of the things that Mother did for him. He misses her most because he needs *somebody to do for*."

We all need *someone to do for*. When that is unfulfilled as a need, we become lonely. In the Lord's own way, Relief Society provides for that need.

Good Neighbor

RUTH G. ROTHE

She did an act of kindness,
In an almost carefree way,
But it made such a difference
As I labored through the day;
My thoughts were optimistic,
My deeds reflected caring.

Oh, the joy that someone starts
Who takes the time for caring.

The Least Among Us

WAYNE B. LYNN

Our small, rented Volkswagen had carried us deep into the interior of central Mexico. We bumped along on this fascinating journey over winding dirt roads through small villages and past clusters of farm homes. Now, as it grew dark, the homes could be seen only by their flickering lights. It was Sunday night and the hour was growing late. The heat of the afternoon lingered in the quiet summer air. We trusted our friend, who was driving and who had lived here before, to find the Church members' home. We had asked him to help us get to know some of the members and to learn more about the country.

A cloud of dust followed us when we finally pulled up beside a tall adobe fence surrounding a dwelling. Our car lights shined on two large metal gates hanging on sturdy hinges. The gates met in the center of the gateway where they were held together with a heavy chain and padlock. We watched in the car lights as our friend, who had been driving, walked to the gate and pounded his fist against the heavy metal. In a few moments the chain was unlocked from the inside, and a short man with a dark complexion opened the gate. He was dressed in black pants, a white short-sleeved shirt, and a black tie. After a moment's pause there was recognition, followed by a wide, spontaneous smile and embrace.

We were soon introduced to him, and he invited us into his humble home. As we walked through the courtyard toward the small, humble dwelling, I noted that a new, more commodious home was under construction nearby. We were greeted at the door by a gracious wife. She too was small in stature. Her raven hair hung in long braids, and her dark eyes sparkled as she smiled and bade us welcome. She was a beautiful quiet woman, her countenance clearly depicting her Lamanite heritage. The room we entered was virtually half of their home. It served as kitchen, dining room, and bedroom. We were invited to sit on the edge of the bed. Our hostess soon presented each of us with a half slice of watermelon. It was a welcome, delicious treat to our thirsty bodies. As we ate I noticed our host had not joined with us and inquired why. I was told that he had just returned from a home teaching visit. The family he had visited was facing some challenges, so he was fasting and praying in their behalf. Our conversation turned to his new home and their progress on its construction. We learned that work on the home had been postponed for the past year because their financial resources and time were directed toward helping build their branch building that had just been completed.

"I guess now that the church is finished you will be able to start working on your house?"

"No. You see, a young man in our branch wants to go on a mission, and we will all be helping finance him. Our home will have to wait."

Tears came to my eyes. I glanced around at the humble surroundings. A small closet held the limited wardrobe for husband and wife. I saw a clean but painfully humble home with no running water, no carpeted floors or soft sofas with matching drapes, no TV or refrigerator, no sink or dishwasher—a home poor in worldly possessions but rich in spirit, a home filled with love sanctified by devotion and sacrifice.

"One day," I thought to myself, "I will want to gain admittance through another gate into the celestial realms on high. I think I will just slip my thumb into the corner of this man's pocket and let him pull me along. When we approach the gate I will smile at the gatekeeper and say, 'I'm with him.'"

An Invitation Through Service

MAX H. MOLGARD

John and Doris Owens had joined the Church in Ireland and had moved to Brigham City, Utah, with their children. The people of Brigham City immediately fell in love with the Owens family. Their love for people and their Irish accents quickly won them a special spot not only in their ward but also throughout the community.

Several years later, John was diagnosed with cancer. As the months wore on he became weaker and more ill. His only regret was that he would not again be able to see the family members he had left in Ireland.

The family was overwhelmed with the financial strain caused by John's sickness. They had no money beyond the payment of the medical bills. One day the family's television stopped working.

A television is important for someone so ill. John had worked at Thiokol Chemical Corporation, and the members of his former carpool now decided to gather money to buy him a new color television. The wives of the men, knowing that others would want to be involved in helping the Owens family, began making some calls. The idea and the money mushroomed.

Soon the Owenses were presented with two tickets to Ireland. They were also given money to spend while they were there. They went to Ireland, visited the relatives, and had a wonderful three weeks.

John passed away two weeks after they returned to Brigham City. Doris still had some of the money that their friends had collected, and when she asked what she should do with the remaining money her friends told her it was hers. They suggested that she stock her shelves with food, but she didn't take that suggestion. Instead she put it away and watched for someone else in need.

Several months later the daughter of a family in the ward became ill with a kidney disease. She would not be well without a kidney transplant. She lived in a city in the East, and her parents longed to be with her but didn't have the money to get there. Doris gladly passed her remaining money on to that family.

She said that she was given so much at the time she and John needed help, and that she would spend the rest of her life looking for ways to help others. Doris felt it was the only way to repay those who had helped her. And she continued to pass it on.

Sources and Permissions

Love and Compassion

" 'I Wuv You' " by Anita R. Canfield, from *Remember, and Perish Not* (Salt Lake City: Bookcraft, 1998), pp. 33–34.

" 'Thou Would Still Be Adored' " by Howard W. Hunter, from *The Teachings of Howard W. Hunter*, ed. Clyde J. Williams (Salt Lake City: Bookcraft, 1997), pp. 134–35.

"A Father's Support" by Marion D. Hanks, from *Bread Upon the Waters* (Salt Lake City: Bookcraft), 1991, p. 158.

"If I Can Stop One Heart from Breaking" by Emily Dickinson, from *Poems by Emily Dickinson,* eds. Mabel Loomis Todd and T. W. Higginson (Boston: Roberts Brothers, 1890), p. 18.

"My Very Dear Sarah," by Sullivan Ballou, letter of 14 July 1861, collections of the Chicago Historical Society. Reprinted by permission of the Chicago Historical Society.

"True Beauty" by Elaine Cannon, from *Bedtime Stories for Grownups* (Salt Lake City: Bookcraft, 1988), pp. 117–18.

"The Only Friend He Ever Had" by George D. Durrant, from *Someone Special—Starring Youth* (Salt Lake City: Bookcraft, 1976), pp. 33–34.

"I Want to Be Your Friend" by Allan K. Burgess and Max H. Molgard, from *Stories That Teach Gospel Principles* (Salt Lake City: Bookcraft, 1989), p. 5–6.

"Love" by Ruth G. Rothe, from *Relief Society Magazine,* August 1968, p. 593.

"Stocking Caps" by Richard M. Siddoway, from *Habits of the Heart* (Salt Lake City: Bookcraft, 1996), pp. 26–33.

Forgiveness

"Bridging the Ditch" by Leland E. Anderson, from *Stories of Power and Purpose* (Salt Lake City: Bookcraft, 1974), pp. 7–9.

" 'To Show Them That Love Is Greater' " by Corrie ten Boom, with John and Elizabeth Sherrill, from *The Hiding Place* (New York: Bantam Books, 1971), pp. 209–10. Used by permission of Chosen Books, Inc., Chappaqua, New York.

"Better Than Revenge" by Glenn Hampton, as quoted in Spencer W. Kimball, *The Miracle of Forgiveness* (Salt Lake City: Bookcraft, 1969), 291–93.

"Love Your Enemies" by Harry Emerson Fosdick, from *Twelve Tests of Character* (New York: George H. Doran Company, 1923), 166–67.

"True Brotherhood" by Richard M. Siddoway, from *Habits of the Heart* (Salt Lake City: Bookcraft, 1996), 60–67.

"But He That Loseth His Life . . ." Name Withheld, as quoted in *Great Teaching Moments,* ed. Kendall Ayres (Salt Lake City: Bookcraft, 1990), pp. 99–101.

"A Man of God" by Elaine Cannon, from *Bedtime Stories for Grownups* (Salt Lake City: Bookcraft, 1988), pp. 9–10.

"Silence" by Neal A. Maxwell, from "Insights from My Life," *1976 Devotional Speeches of the Year* (Provo: Brigham Young University Press, 1977), pp. 187–201. Used by permission.

"Roses Are Red" by Richard M. Siddoway, from *Twelve Tales of Christmas* (Salt Lake City: Bookcraft, 1992), pp. 15–23.

Home and Family

"The Long Embrace" by Randal A. Wright, from *Eternal Families,* ed., Douglas E. Brinley and Daniel K Judd (Salt Lake City: Bookcraft, 1996), pp. 179–80.

" 'I Loved Your Father' " by Elaine Cannon, from *Mothering* (Salt Lake City: Bookcraft, 1993), p. 43.

"The Boy Is Worth More Than the Cow" by Wayne B. Lynn, from *Lessons from Life* (Salt Lake City: Bookcraft, 1987), 79–81.

"On Goals" by Evalyn D. Bennett, from Elaine Cannon, *Mothering* (Salt Lake City: Bookcraft, 1993), pp. 129–32.

"A Father Reading the Bible" by Felicia Dorothea Browne Hemans, from *The Poetical Works of Mrs. Hemans* (New York: Thomas Y. Crowell & Co., 18?), p. 429.

"Watching Katie" by George D. Durrant, from *Love at Home—Starring Grandpa* (Salt Lake City: Bookcraft, 1995), pp. 43–45.

"Dad Will Come" by Ardeth G. Kapp, from "Young Women Striving Together," *Ensign,* November 1984, pp. 96–97. © 1998 by Intellectual Reserve, Inc. Used by permission.

"As Children See Us" by Bryant S. Hinckley, from . . . *Not By Bread Alone* (Salt Lake City: Bookcraft, 1955), p. 84.

" 'I Am Waiting for You' " by Marion D. Hanks, from *The Gift of Self* (Salt Lake City: Bookcraft, 1974), pp. 289–90.

"The Perfect Dinner Table" by Edgar A. Guest, from *A Heap o' Livin'* (Chicago: The Reilly & Britton Co., 1916), pp. 118–19.

"Proposal" by Muriel Jenkins Heal, from *Relief Society Magazine,* April 1965, p. 284.

"Do Unto Others" by Richard M. Siddoway, from *Mom—and Other Great Women I've Known* (Salt Lake City: Bookcraft, 1994), pp. 68–82.

" 'Grandpa, Are You Awake?' " by George D. Durrant, from *Love at Home—Starring Grandpa* (Salt Lake City: Bookcraft, 1995), pp. 1–3.

Faith and Trust

"The Boy and the Mango Tree" by John H. Groberg, from *In the Eye of the Storm* (Salt Lake City: Bookcraft, 1993), pp. 49–53.

"The Gardener and the Currant Bush" by Hugh B. Brown, from *Eternal Quest,* ed. Charles Manley Brown (Salt Lake City: Bookcraft, 1956), pp. 243–46.

"Drinking That Water Will Mean Death!" by Charles R. Woodbury, as quoted in *Stories of Insight and Inspiration,* comp., Margie Calhoun Jensen (Salt Lake City: Bookcraft, 1976), pp. 231–32.

"His House" by C. S. Lewis, from *Mere Christianity* (New York: Macmillan Publishing Co., 1952), p. 174.

" 'Walk to the Edge of the Light' " by Boyd K. Packer, from *The Holy Temple* (Salt Lake City: Bookcraft, 1980), pp. 184–85.

"About His Father's Business" by Leland E. Anderson, from *Stories of Power and Purpose* (Salt Lake City: Bookcraft, 1974), pp. 10–11.

" 'Ko E Maama E' " by John H. Groberg, from *In the Eye of the Storm* (Salt Lake City: Bookcraft, 1993), pp. 182–84.

"Hezekiah Mitchell: 'I Knew That Faith Must Prevail' " by Garrett H. Garff. Previously unpublished.

"Strong, Like the Pioneers" by Bruce Newbold, from *In Our Fathers' Footsteps* (Salt Lake City: Bookcraft, 1998), pp. 98–102.

"Faith in the Tongan Islands" by Eric Shumway, from *Stories of Insight and Inspiration,* comp., Margie Calhoun Jensen (Salt Lake City: Bookcraft, 1976), pp. 71–73.

"The Little Blind Boy of Holland" by Osborne J. P. Widtsoe, from *LDS Stories of Faith and Courage,* comp., Preston Nibley (Salt Lake City: Bookcraft, 1957), pp. 105–8.

Prayer

" 'Sh-h-h, Grandfather, I'm Listening' " by Elaine Cannon, from *Bedtime Stories for Grownups* (Salt Lake City: Bookcraft, 1988), p. 12.

"Beth's Birthday Present" by Allan K. Burgess, from *Teach Me to Walk in the Light* (Salt Lake City: Bookcraft, 1995), pp. 17–19.

"The Lord's Wind" by John H. Groberg, from *In the Eye of the Storm* (Salt Lake City: Bookcraft, 1993), pp. 198–201.

" 'I Know He Won't Catch Anything' " by Boyd K. Packer, from *Let Not Your Heart be Troubled* (Salt Lake City: Bookcraft, 1991), p. 96.

"A Message from the Heart" by C. Steven Hatch, from *Stories of Insight and Inspiration,* comp., Margie Calhoun Jensen (Salt Lake City: Bookcraft, 1976), pp. 118–21.

"George Washington Prays at Valley Forge" by Mason Weems, from *A History of the Life and Death, Virtues and Exploits of General George Washington* (New York: Macy-Masius, 1927), pp. 300–301.

"She Expected an Answer" by Sarah H. Bradford, from *Harriet Tubman: The Moses of Her People* (New York: G. R. Lockwood & Son, 1886), pp. 52–57.

" 'Pray for Her' " by Anita R. Canfield, from *Remember, and Perish Not* (Salt Lake City: Bookcraft, 1998), pp. 74–75.

Humility and Obedience

"A Different Kind of Courage" by Wayne B. Lynn, from *Lessons from Life* (Salt Lake City: Bookcraft, 1987), pp. 50–52.

" 'Only God Gives A's' " by Brett G. London, *Ensign,* March 1988, pp. 55–56. © 1998 by Intellectual Reserve, Inc. Used by permission.

"Humility Is Royalty Without a Crown" by Spencer W. Kimball, *Improvement Era* 66 (August 1963): 656–59, 704.

"Lesson at the Gas Pump" by Randal A. Wright. A version of this story appeared in *Latter-day Digest,* January 1993, pp. 63–65.

"The Long Walk" by Marion D. Hanks, from *Bread Upon the Waters* (Salt Lake City: Bookcraft, 1991), pp. 91–94.

"The Parable of the Unwise Bee" by James E. Talmage, *Improvement Era* 17 (September 1914): 1008–9.

"Putting the Kingdom of God First" by Rex Paul Greenwood, from *Stories of Insight and Inspiration,* comp. Margie Calhoun Jensen (Salt Lake City: Bookcraft, 1976), pp. 215–17.

"True Nobility" by Edgar A. Guest, from *A Heap 'o Livin'* (Chicago: The Reilly & Britton Co., 1916), p. 91.

"High Standards Attract" by Boyd K. Packer, from *Memorable Stories and Parables by Boyd K. Packer* (Salt Lake City: Bookcraft, 1997), pp. 31–32.

The Workings of the Spirit

"The Cross-Country Flight" by Kris Mackay, from *In Loving Hands* (Salt Lake City: Bookcraft, 1985), pp. 62–67.

"Hearken to the Spirit" by Bruce R. McConkie, *The Friend,* September 1972, pp. 10–11. Used by permission.

"Find Her" by Allan K. Burgess and Max H. Molgard, from *Stories That Teach Gospel Principles* (Salt Lake City: Bookcraft, 1989), pp. 59–61.

"A Visit in the Rain" by Kris Mackay, from *In Loving Hands* (Salt Lake City: Bookcraft, 1985), pp. 107–10.

"Leave for West Berlin Today" by Dieter Berndt, from *Stories of Insight and Inspiration,* comp. Margie Calhoun Jensen (Salt Lake City: Bookcraft, 1976), pp. 115–18.

"Jesus, Listening, Can Hear" by Jean Ernstrom, from Bruce and Joyce Erickson, *When Life Doesn't Seem Fair* (Salt Lake City: Bookcraft, 1995), pp. 50–53.

"That Is the Worst Lesson I've Ever Heard!" by Allan K. Burgess and Max H. Molgard, from *Stories That Teach Gospel Principles* (Salt Lake City: Bookcraft, 1989), pp. 17–19.

" 'We've Been Waiting for You' " by Grant H. Taylor. Previously unpublished.

"Physical Riches in Exchange for a Covenant Family" by Allan K. Burgess, from *New Insights into the Old Testament* (Salt Lake City: Bookcraft, 1993), pp. 75–76.

Teaching by Example

"Mr. Brimhall" by George D. Durrant, from *Look at the Sky* (Salt Lake City: Bookcraft, 1994), pp. 14–16.

"What Religion Can Produce a Young Man like That?" by Marion D. Hanks, from *Bread Upon the Waters* (Salt Lake City: Bookcraft, 1991), pp. 135–36.

"Example Opened the Door" by Kevin Stoker, from *Missionary Moments* (Salt Lake City: Bookcraft, 1989), pp. 74–75.

"Caught Speeding" by S. Dilworth Young, from "Living Flames, Not Dead Ashes," *1977 Devotional Speeches of the Year* (Provo: Brigham Young University Press, 1978), pp. 95–101. Copyright © by Brigham Young University, Publications & Graphics. Reprinted by permission.

"Jimmy" by George D. Durrant, from *Look at the Sky* (Salt Lake City: Bookcraft, 1994), pp. 88–91.

"Joseph Smith Teaches Justice and Mercy" by Truman G. Madsen, from *Joseph Smith the Prophet* (Salt Lake City: Bookcraft, 1989), p. 61.

"The Hunting Trip" by John Covey, from Michaelene Grassli, Dean Packer, and Steve Woodhead, *Dad, You're the Best!* (Salt Lake City: Bookcraft, 1994), p.14.

Courage

" 'Norman the Mormon' " by Allan K. Burgess, from *Becoming a Celestial Person in a Telestial World* (Salt Lake City: Bookcraft, 1990), p. 55.

"The Faith of a Mormon Girl" by Elizabeth Claridge McCune, from "Elizabeth Claridge McCune," *Utah Genealogical and Historical Magazine,* Vol. 16, pp. 1–7.

"1,300 Degrees Fahrenheit" by Marion D. Hanks, from *The Gift of Self* (Salt Lake City: Bookcraft, 1974), pp. 81–82.

"Rock-Throwing Lessons" by Kevin Stoker, from *Missionary Moments* (Salt Lake City: Bookcraft, 1989), pp. 5–7.

"Richard Kirkland, the Humane Hero of Fredericksburg" by General J. B. Kershaw, *Southern Historical Society Papers* 8 (January-December 1880): 186–88.

"Prayers of Courage" by Anita R. Canfield, from *Remember, and Perish Not* (Salt Lake City: Bookcraft, 1998), pp. 23–58.

"If It Is to Be It Is Up to Me" by George D. Durrant, from *Someone Special—Starring Youth* (Salt Lake City: Bookcraft, 1976), pp. 48–54.

"His Own Mind" by Marion D. Hanks, from *Now and Forever* (Salt Lake City: Bookcraft, 1974), pp. 5–6.

Happiness and Gratitude

"Because I Have Been Given Much" by Richard M. Siddoway, from *Mom—and Other Great Women I've Known* (Salt Lake City: Bookcraft, 1994), pp. 83–91.

" 'I Feel Sorry for Him' " by John H. Groberg, from *In the Eye of the Storm* (Salt Lake City: Bookcraft, 1993), pp. 131–34.

" 'Thank You for the Fleas' " by Corrie ten Boom, with John and Elizabeth Sherril, from *The Hiding Place* (New York: Bantam Books, 1971), pp. 196–99, 208–9. Used by permission of Chosen Books, Inc., Chappaqua, New York.

"My Little Bread and Butter Life" by Catherine B. Pratt, *Relief Society Magazine,* January 1966, p. 41.

"Dad's Gratitude" by H. David Burton, from "Heroes," *Ensign,* May 1993, p. 47. © 1998 by Intellectual Reserve, Inc. Used by permission.

"Eliza Roxcy Snow and Seeing the 'Better Side' " by Garrett H. Garff. Previously unpublished.

" 'I Can Feel Just as Well as Anybody' " by George Albert Smith, in Conference Report, October 1947, pp. 7–8.

"Miguel Had No Shoes" by Allan K. Burgess and Max H. Molgard, from *The Gospel in Action* (Salt Lake City: Bookcraft, 1992), pp.117–18.

"A Poor Memory" by Richard M. Siddoway, from *Habits of the Heart* (Salt Lake City: Bookcraft, 1996), pp. 34–43.

Service and Sacrifice

"Lord, Make Me an Instrument of Your Peace" by St. Francis of Assisi, from John Bartlett, *Bartlett's Familiar Quotations* (Boston: Little, Brown and Company, 1968), p. 157.

"You Never Know Who You May Save" by Jacob de Jager, from "You Never Know Who You May Save," *Ensign,* November 1976, pp. 56–57. © 1998 by Intellectual Reserve, Inc. Used by permission.

"Gospel Givers" by Leland E. Anderson, from *Stories of Power and Purpose* (Salt Lake City: Bookcraft, 1974), pp. 68–70.

"Nadine's Dance" by Grant H. Taylor. Previously unpublished.

"Someone to Do For" by Boyd K. Packer, from *Memorable Stories and Parables by Boyd K. Packer* (Salt Lake City: Bookcraft, 1997), p. 87.

"Good Neighbor" by Ruth G. Rothe, from *Relief Society Magazine,* October 1968, p. 755.

"The Least Among Us" by Wayne B. Lynn, from *Lessons from Life* (Salt Lake City: Bookcraft, 1987), pp. 59–61.

"An Invitation Through Service" by Max H. Molgard, from *Inviting the Spirit into Our Lives* (Salt Lake City: Bookcraft, 1993), pp. 19–20.

In the works are plans to publish additional volumes of *Sunshine for the Latter-day Saint Soul*. Bookcraft invites readers to contribute to the collection of literature from which stories for subsequent volumes will be selected.

Stories may be up to 1,500 words in length and must reflect Latter-day Saint values and principles, as well as uplift and inspire readers. If you have such a story, take the time to write it down. Likewise, encourage others who may have uplifting stories to write them down and submit them. All stories will be subject to editorial review.

Send your stories to:

Sunshine for the Latter-day Saint Soul
2405 West Orton Circle
West Valley City, UT 84119
Fax: 801-908-3401
E-mail: sunshine@ldsworld.com

Please include your name, address, and a daytime phone number with all submissions.